# UNLOCKING THE POWER

## of Academic Vocabulary with
### Secondary English Language Learners

## Yu Ren Dong

Maupin House *by*
# capstone®
professional

Cover design: Studio Montage
Book design: Mickey Cuthbertson

Dong, Yu Ren.
Unlocking the power of academic vocabulary with secondary english
language learners / Yu Ren Dong.
    p. cm.
 Includes bibliographical references and index.
 ISBN 978-1-934338-93-3 (pbk.)
 1. Vocabulary—Problems, exercises, etc. 2.  English language--Study
and teaching (Secondary—Foreign speakers.  I. Title.
 PE1449.D654 201
 428.2'40712--dc22
                        2010051500

Parts of the book come from sources listed below. I am grateful for permission to use the following materials:

Page xiv. Paragraph appeared in *Educational Leadership, 62* (4), 14-19 (2004-2005), written by Yu Ren Dong. "Learning to think in English." Published by ASCD.

Pages 12-13. Paragraph appeared in *Educational Leadership, 66* (7), 26-31 (2009), written by Yu Ren Dong. "Linking to prior learning." Published by ASCD.

Page 17. Paragraph appeared in *Educational Leadership, 64* (2), 22-27 (2004-2005), written by Yu Ren Dong. "Getting at the content." Published by ASCD.

Page 17. Diagram appeared in *Contemporary Educational Psychology, 29* (3), 230-247 (2004), written by Nita A. Paris and Shawn M. Glynn. "Elaborate analogies in science text: Tools for enhancing preservice teachers' knowledge and attitudes." Published by Elsevier.

Page 22. Dialogues appeared in *English Journal, 93* (4), 29-35 (2004), written by Yu Ren Dong. "Don't keep them in the dark: Teaching metaphorical language to English language learners." Published by NCTE.

Pages 24-25. Dialogue and reflection appeared in *International Journal of Bilingual Education and Bilingualism, 5* (1), 40-57 (2002), written by Yu Ren Dong. "Integrating language and content: How three biology teachers work with non-English speaking students." Published by Taylor & Francis.

Pages 44-46. Teacher's reflection and dialogue appeared in *Teaching language and content to linguistically and culturally diverse students: Principles, ideas, and materials*, 67-68 and 99-100 (2004), written by Yu Ren Dong. Published by Information Age Publishing.

Page 74. Dialogue appeared *Educational Leadership, 62* (4), 14-19 (2004-2005), written by Yu Ren Dong, "Getting at the content." Published by ASCD.

Pages 91-92. Poem appeared in *Journal of Adolescent & Adult Literacy, 51* (2), 98-111 (2007), written by Jacobson, J., Lapp, D., & Flood, J. "A seven-step instructional plan for teaching English-language learners to comprehend and use homonyms, homophones, and homographs" Published by IRA.

Maupin House publishes professional resources for K-12 educators. Contact us for tailored, in-school training or to schedule an author for a workshop or conference. Visit www.maupinhouse.com for free lesson plan downloads.

Maupin House by
capstone
professional

Maupin House Publishing, Inc. by capstone Professional
1710 Roe Crest Drive
North Mankato, MN 56003
www.maupinhouse.com
888-262-6135
info@maupinhouse.com

021916  009531R

# *Dedication*

To my mother, Jin Qun Zhu, whose feisty and loving spirit, talent for teaching,
and unfaltering belief in my ability has inspired me with a love for teaching and learning.

# TABLE OF CONTENTS

• • • • •

# LIST OF TABLES

• • • • •

# LIST OF FIGURES

•••••

# ACKNOWLEDGMENTS

• • • • •

My very grateful thanks go out to all the in-service and pre-service teachers in my graduate-level Language, Literacy, and Culture in Education; Multicultural Literature; and Methods of Teaching English in Middle and High School classes, and their students who used the vocabulary strategies represented in this book. I'm blessed with the opportunity to work with them in developing and field-testing those strategies. Their enthusiasm and outstanding efforts and creation make those vocabulary strategies exciting, meaningful, and relevant in a wider range of classrooms.

I would also like to thank my family. My husband has supported my professional pursuits over the years and helped with the design of those graphics to showcase the vocabulary-teaching strategies. My son has been my first copy editor of my writing all these years. His excellent English language skills, firsthand knowledge of language, and subject-matter knowledge learned in New York City public schools added clarity, accuracy, and extra credibility to my manuscript.

The vocabulary ideas developed and strategies highlighted here have evolved over the years. Some have appeared in my articles published in *Educational Leadership, English Journal, International Journal of Bilingual Education and Bilingualism,* and in my book *Teaching Language and Content to Linguistically and Culturally Diverse Students: Principles, Ideas, and Materials.*

# INTRODUCTION

• • • • •

*Without grammar very little can be conveyed; without*
*vocabulary nothing can be conveyed.*
—David Wilkins

• • • • •

*I am fascinated by language in daily life. I spend a great deal of time*
*thinking about the power of language—the way it can evoke an emotion,*
*a visual image, a complex idea, or a simple truth.*
— Amy Tan

Most secondary teachers in all subjects understand the critical role that vocabulary plays in understanding subject matter and developing literacy skills. But learning vocabulary encompasses more than memorizing words. When a student learns words like *photosynthesis, foreshadowing, colonies, variable,* and *advertising,* she learns the concepts behind the words as well as the actual definitions, spelling, and sounds. The concept becomes part of conversation, reading, writing, and thinking in all subject areas.

Thus, effective vocabulary instruction must also encompass teaching about the concepts that are an inseparable part of words. Discipline-specific concepts are constructed, communicated, understood, and expressed by words; secondary-level ELLs must have that vocabulary in order to think critically and creatively. In studying the challenges of teaching discipline-specific vocabulary to secondary students, researchers found that a thorough understanding of the vocabulary used to express important concepts is a prerequisite for learning any subject (Bialystok, 2008; Graves, 1987; Harmon & Hedrick, 2005).

English language learners understand the importance of learning academic vocabulary. But their need is more urgent because time is not on their side. On average, an ELL requires five to seven years to catch up with his native English-speaking peers in the content-area vocabulary so necessary for academic success in the classroom, on tests, and for graduation (Colliers, 1987; Fisher & Frey, 2008; Freeman & Freeman, 2009; Nagy, 1988; Nation, 1990; Snow, 2008).

The conversation that follows illustrates several typical ELLs' views toward vocabulary learning in secondary schools:

> "There are so many new words in the reading and in class discussions. I often use my Chinese-English electronic translator to understand them. But if there are too many, I have a hard time keeping up. I feel like I missed a lot in class."
> —A ninth-grade Chinese-American student

> "Words are important. I envy those American students who speak with slang and idiomatic usages. I want to talk with them, but I don't have the language."
> —An eighth-grade Mexican-American student

> "Only my ESL teacher teaches vocabulary. When I go to other classes, teachers don't teach it. I really want to improve my vocabulary to pass the Regents Exams."
> —A tenth-grade Ecuadorian-American student

> "Reading biology is most difficult for me because there are so many new words, and I have to look them up in the dictionary."
> —A ninth-grade Korean-American student

Maria, a ninth-grade science teacher, highlights the urgency that ELL students feel about succeeding in vocabulary acquisition (Dong, 2004/2005):

> "In my classroom, I have students who are placed in ESL classes, and students who are newly mainstreamed. Those students who do not understand the language are usually sitting in class with blank looks on their faces. Some of them try to make sense of the words by using electronic translators during the lesson. The students who try to do this usually get behind in the lesson and will only understand half of the day's material. On the next day, these students are starting further back in the material than their English-speaking peers and end up lost in the curriculum. What should I do to help these students?" (14)

Maria's concerns reflect those shared by many mainstream subject-matter teachers across the board—from art and music, physical education, home economics, and health to core academic subjects. The common message is clear: in order for ELLs to understand challenging academic work at the secondary level, subject-matter teachers like Maria must teach vocabulary explicitly and on a regular basis.

Over the years, I have worked with many secondary ELLs and their subject-matter teachers to find ways to increase concept-based vocabulary acquisition. My survey of subject-matter textbooks used in mainstreamed New York City public high schools has shown a tremendous demand for learning disciplinary-specific vocabulary at the secondary level. All agree academic and disciplinary-specific vocabulary plays a critical role in learning academic knowledge.

My review of high school curricula documents the number of commonly used words used in secondary classrooms and illustrates the challenge for secondary ELLS. Lists of those words are found in the various appendices of this book.

**Table 1: Secondary Subject-matter Vocabulary Counts**

| Subject | Number of Words to Learn |
|---|---|
| Academic words used in the classroom | 556 (See Appendix A) |
| Biology | 1,215 (See Appendix B) |
| General sciences | 466 (See Appendix C) |
| English language arts | 186 (See Appendix D) |
| Mathematics | 480 (See Appendix E) |
| U.S. history | 524 (See Appendix F) |
| World history | 1,481 (See Appendix G) |
| **Total** | **4,908** |

Obviously, all those words cannot be learned purposefully and fully unless teachers provide explicit and regular vocabulary instruction beyond merely teaching the word itself. The concepts underlying those words must also be taught.

# Typical Vocabulary Instruction in Secondary Schools

David, an eleventh-grade ELL student, sits in his English class reading *To Kill a Mockingbird* by Harper Lee. For homework the day before, the teacher had assigned ten vocabulary words from the book which would become the focus for today's lesson. These ten words were *assuage, taciturn, tyrannical, inequity, fractious, predilection, amble, phantom, guile,* and *auspicious*.

The teacher asked the students to give the dictionary definition. Students were not very involved, and she had to call on students herself to elicit answers. Afterward, she asked the students to come up with synonyms for the assigned words, writing them beside the vocabulary on the board like this:

assuage = lessen
taciturn = antisocial
tyrannical = mean
inequity = unfairness
fractious = unruly
predilection = love
amble = stroll
phantom = ghost
guile = slyness
auspicious = lucky

The teacher then asked the class to copy down the words to prepare for the end-of-week vocabulary quiz. Throughout the lesson, David was quiet and had little interaction with the teacher or his peers. He seemed to be very busy. He copied down everything on the board carefully, and he listened to his peers when they gave out definitions. He did not seem to understand most of the vocabulary or the synonyms, however, even after translating them with his bilingual electronic translator. David revealed that he felt overwhelmed. When asked why he used his bilingual translator, he said that he didn't understand the definitions given by his peers since many of these definitions also contain new words he didn't understand.

The scenario just described is typical of how "conventional wisdom" says that vocabulary instruction should be handled in mainstream subject-matter classes—through dictionary searches and memorization. The teacher instructs students to consult the dictionary or glossary for definitions and synonyms and asks them to memorize them for the exam. The method often disengages students from active learning and reduces their interest in language to simple fill-ins and rote memorization with limited thinking involved.

Although researchers have already shown the problems and ineffectiveness of traditional vocabulary instruction, many teachers continue to use this approach because of curricular constraints and misconceptions. At the secondary level, teachers assume students will take care of vocabulary in their own time or already understand the vocabulary appropriate to the lesson. . Teachers don't understand that their success in teaching subject-matter knowledge to a large extent rests on how successful they are in teaching vocabulary in a rich and meaningful way.

Understandably, teachers are so busy covering the curriculum and preparing students for standardized tests that they don't set aside time in class for an open discussion of vocabulary concepts.

The result? Vocabulary development is viewed as a supplement to learning subject-matter material instead of an important tool to acquire that knowledge.

It's also true that while subject-matter teachers certainly know their discipline-specific vocabulary, few understand how to effectively teach concept-based vocabulary to their students, especially to students who are still learning English. Many have not been trained in ELL-specific instructional skills. And while advocating wide reading and incidental vocabulary learning are good ideas to a certain extent, they are not enough.

Secondary students still need in-depth experiences with learning key discipline-specific vocabulary in order to make those words their own. And if the traditional methods of vocabulary teaching are inadequate for native English-speaking students – as research points out – how much more detrimental are they for ELLS who have to close a severe word-deficiency gap in a limited amount of time?

# What This Book Covers

ELLs need a systematic, meaningful, contextualized, and exciting way to learn and use vocabulary. *Unlocking the Power of Academic Vocabulary with Secondary English Language Learners* describes and illustrates strategies that will help secondary teachers expand their instructional repertoires for teaching academic and disciplinary-specific vocabulary to ELLs. It provides easy-to-integrate activities for every secondary subject-matter teacher.

The first chapter provides an overview of general principles and strategies used for effective vocabulary instruction in subject-matter classes for ELLs, as well as a description of the unique challenges that ELLs face in learning vocabulary. I also delineate specific ingredients for effective vocabulary instruction, such as how to select the word for instruction, how to plan, and how to teach vocabulary.

Chapters Two, Three, Four, and Five offer examples of effective vocabulary instruction based on those principles and strategies. Within each chapter, I describe and illustrate specific vocabulary instructional activities developed around the principles and strategies. For each activity, I include an explanation about the importance of and need for the activity, how the activity works, and examples of the activity.

Various appendices provide lists of subject-matter specific vocabulary suggested for student mastery.

As technology is a part of our everyday life, it should be used for vocabulary teaching and learning as well. The combined visual, audio, and interactive nature of many Internet vocabulary websites and texts, as well as computer software, provides interesting and rich opportunities for ELLs' vocabulary development. As many secondary ELLs are catching up very fast when it comes to the Internet, computers, electronic gadgets, etc., technology becomes a friendly and motivating resource to use for vocabulary development. You will find many activities described in this book that have utilized technology in one way or another and that fit well into your classroom. Many schools have interactive whiteboards and computer rooms with Internet connections. Even composing simple emails, writing using a word processor, or accessing free dictionaries, thesauruses, magazines, and newspapers online can enhance students' vocabulary and reading and writing skills. Interdisciplinary opportunities are endless when the Internet is used effectively. Students can always find varied versions of a text, gather information on topics written in multiple levels of language proficiencies, select materials of their choice, learn concepts and words, and compose visually rich writing.

# CHAPTER 1
## Effective Vocabulary Instruction for ELLs

• • • • •

*What I hear I forget,*
*What I see I remember,*
*What I do I understand.*
— *A Chinese saying*

What are some of the unique challenges for and needs of English language learners as they learn academic vocabulary? First, as mentioned before, these students are not on an equal vocabulary playing field with their native English-speaking peers. They don't have the background of cultural knowledge or rich oral language or a basic repertoire of English academic and discipline-specific vocabulary attained during formative years. In fact, many are still in the process of learning English for both basic interpersonal communication skills (BICS) and cognitive academic language proficiency (CALPS) (Cummins, 1984).

Even ELLs who have been in a U.S. school for a while and achieved fluency in BICS and have gone through school in their home countries still need quite a few years to catch up with their native peers in terms of CALPS.

These students also face an enormous gap in the size of their vocabularies compared with those of their native English-speaking peers. Conservatively speaking, native English-speaking students begin their school already knowing about 2,000 words. By high school, these students should have learned about 12,000 words in school (Nagy, 1984; Nation, 2006). In comparison, ELLs who come to secondary schools have to begin learning vocabulary from scratch. They need to acquire a sufficient vocabulary size while their academic clocks keep ticking.

Research has shown that a lack of vocabulary size and knowledge is one of the major reasons for significant discrepancies in reading proficiency and standardized test performance between native English speakers and ELLs. This gap creates serious consequences for lower performance on tests and graduation rates, and it highlights the need for explicit, integrated, and systematic vocabulary instruction as part of teaching subject-matter knowledge.

Let's take the word *propaganda*, for example. Most native English-speaking students have already repeatedly encountered the concept of propaganda from elementary school days as well as from media and pop culture. They have established culturally relevant background knowledge about the concept that generally contains a negative connotation. A high school social studies teacher may not understand or feel the need to teach this basic concept behind the word. Instead, he believes his job is not to define the concepts behind the word, but to use it as part of the academic unit under study.

Yet English language learners may not have any background knowledge or basic understanding of the connotations this word carries in English. In Chinese, for example, the word *propaganda* has the meaning of passing on information with only good connotations, which is certainly not congruent with the prior knowledge that the teacher has in mind when teaching about propaganda used by Nazis in WWII. Therefore, subject-matter teachers must be mindful about these possible mismatches and differences in ELLs' prior learning and be prepared to teach not only the word but also the concept and assumptions that the word carries.

The good news is that subject-matter teachers usually can tap into students' prior knowledge and transfer the conceptual knowledge from the native culture if they provide opportunities to scaffold those transfers. Several researchers (Cummins, 1984; Genesee, 1994), in fact, have argued for interdependence in the development of conceptual knowledge between L1 (native language) and L2 (second language).

The existing conceptual system in the student's native language serves as a "cognitive hanger" on which new vocabulary can be hung. Once these overlaps are identified, English language learners do not need to learn the new concept all over again; instead, they just need to learn how to switch the label of the concept from their native language to English. For example, an immigrant student who arrives at an American high school may have already acquired the concept of *adaptation* in his or her native language or through his or her life and immigrant experiences. So the student may only need to acquire a new label in L2 for an already acquired concept.

## What Kind of Vocabulary to Teach

Secondary teachers must, of course, know and teach their subject matter's vocabulary. But effective vocabulary instruction at this level also requires the teacher to know their ELLs' prior education, native languages, cultural backgrounds, etc. The first step is examining curriculum for vocabulary instruction opportunities that take into account the students' academic and cultural backgrounds, their native language, and the demands of subject-matter curricula and language.

In secondary schools, teachers deal with two types of vocabulary on a daily basis: academic and discipline specific. Academic vocabulary includes those words used in classroom discussions, teacher questions, students' writings, test questions, etc. Examples of academic vocabulary are words and phrases like *support your argument, define the concept, describe the cause-effect relationship, give the approximate square root*, etc. ELLs must learn these words to understand class discussions and perform well on tests and writing assignments.

These words can be easily identified and should be taught on a regular basis in all subject-matter classes. Teachers should not assume that these students have already learned these words in their schools back home. There is no guarantee, even with ELLs who had schooling back in their home countries, that they have acquired these basic academic words and phrases.

It's wise to remember that academic vocabulary varies from culture to culture. For example, the word *argument* is a commonly used academic word in American classrooms; however, it is not used in the same way in other cultures, such as China. So the Western thought patterns such as *prove your point* and *support your argument with evidence and textual references* may be foreign to students coming from other cultures. Without a clear understanding of what argument means and how it is valued in American culture, these students could not participate in classroom discussions or write an effective argumentative essay.

Discipline-specific vocabulary is vocabulary that students learn when studying a specific subject matter in the subject-matter class. Examples are *trigonometry*, *bisector*, and *hypotenuse* in mathematics; *reaction*, *solution*, *burning*, and *energy* in chemistry; *foreshadowing*, *characterization*, *plot*, and *omniscient narrator* in English; *autocrat*, *propaganda*, *democracy*, and *checks and balances* in social studies, etc. These words have specific meanings in a specific discipline even though some of them can be used in other disciplines or in everyday English.

These words carry with them concepts which cannot be separated from content knowledge. Discipline-specific vocabulary enables us to talk, think, and express the subject-matter content knowledge; and subject content knowledge governs, shapes, and extends discipline-specific vocabulary. Simply teaching a new word's meaning is not enough.

Most secondary teachers do not consider their lessons to be vocabulary lessons. Yet content knowledge is tightly interwoven with knowledge about vocabulary, enabling students to read, talk, and think in mathematics, sciences, English, social studies, history, and art. Vocabulary teaching and subject-matter teaching go hand in hand (Bialystok, 2008; Harmon & Hedrick, 2005).

By knowing the two important sets of vocabulary for secondary ELLs to learn—academic and discipline-specific vocabulary—subject-matter teachers can consider the following aspects of word study besides word meaning in their instruction:

- The culturally specific conceptual system that defines and governs the word
- The feelings and attitudes of the word (connotation)
- The functional use of the word: how the word is combined with other words in the context
- The relationship between the word and other words that share similar meanings
- Structure of the word: parts of speech, how the word is formed and evolved
- Metaphorical language and multiple meanings of the word

Vocabulary instruction at the secondary level requires an in-depth word study for meaningful communication and productive word use. The six aspects of vocabulary instruction mentioned previously are geared towards meeting the needs of second-language learners, and they provide a rich and engaging context for learning new vocabulary. Teaching all six aspects explicitly integrates vocabulary teaching with subject-matter instruction.

Finally, vocabulary learning for ELLs encompasses learning about American culture and the Western conceptual system. This includes not only the words used to think and discuss content knowledge but also the ways the classroom discussion is orchestrated, ideas and performance are valued and expectations, and standards are set.

## Preparing for Vocabulary Instruction

Planning is crucial for any subject-matter teacher who is about to begin a new topic of study or a new reading passage that contains new vocabulary/concepts. But, first things first: know your ELL students. The prior knowledge that your ELLs bring to your classroom definitely influences your instruction.

**Activate prior knowledge first.** Effective vocabulary instruction begins with including students' prior knowledge and making the learning task relevant to their lives (Marzano, 2004; Dong, 2004, 2006, 2009). Discipline-specific vocabulary/concepts at the secondary level often require students to have certain background knowledge from their earlier schooling or exposure to American popular culture.

For example, before teaching the concept of *legislation*, the teacher can assume that native English speakers have already had social studies lessons on this topic in their upper-elementary school and middle school and they have experienced the process of legislation through watching TV and reading newspapers. This may not be true for ELLs, who might not have even heard the word before.

Exploring prior knowledge about government and lawmaking becomes the departure point to teach the vocabulary/concept purposefully and meaningfully. A short questionnaire, writing assignment, or open discussion about the prior knowledge at the beginning of the lesson is helpful to learn what students know. Using cognates (words with similar spelling and meaning across languages) is an effective way to introduce the new word in English for ELLS whose native language is from the Romance language family.

**Bridge prior knowledge with learning.** Use surveys, informal writing assignments, or questions to gauge students' prior knowledge in relation to the teaching topic or concept at hand. If the teacher learns that his or her ELLs do not have much prior knowledge on this topic due to the differences in their native cultures, education, and political systems, the teacher then can strategize how to backtrack to teach the basic concepts about the word first—before teaching the lesson that incorporates the word.

**Establish a positive learning atmosphere.** A classroom designed to support students allows you to take advantage of collaborative learning opportunities that combine native English speakers with ELLs. A work group composed of native English speakers and ELLs can, for example, design a vocabulary glossary that includes definitions from all the group's languages. In collaborative learning arrangements, students learn how to communicate with and learn from each other.

**Select a few words at a time to teach.** Although it is tempting to include many new words in a single lesson, research has shown that teachers who focus on five to seven new words at a time often gain better results in teaching vocabulary for better understanding and retention.

The subject-matter teacher should choose the most relevant words to the lesson, the conceptual words, and words used with high frequency in a subject matter and class (Nation, 2006, 2008). Go over the curriculum and reading materials for possible unfamiliar words and, before teaching, conduct an informal survey to explore whether students understand the concepts or words. Keep a balance between the number of new words to teach and student need for learning those words.

On the one hand, you want students to approach the topic or reading with excitement and curiosity, so don't give out too many word definitions and pre-teach so long that an engaging learning session becomes a boring memorization drill. On the other hand, you don't want to gloss over the new vocabulary concepts embedded in the reading. At this stage, you should establish an adventurous learning atmosphere that still supports students according to their needs.

**Present new words in engaging ways.** Rather than presenting new words in alphabetical or chronological order, research supports presenting new words around a common theme and relating those words to words that students already know (Blachowicz, et al., 2006; Howard, 1999; Hudelson & Rigg, 1994-1995; Loughran, 2005; Saunders & Goldenberg, 1999). Awareness of educational backgrounds, native languages, and level of proficiency of English are all critical to presenting new vocabulary in a meaningful and appropriate way.

Visuals, audios, and even physical movements engage students and support the acquisition of new vocabulary. Using multilingual glossaries or cognates, present new words using students' native languages. Although some teachers may be hesitant to use ELLs' native languages in class, when used to support instruction in English, translations or cognates can quickly get meaning across and illuminate the concepts which might be difficult to explain by using English only (Thornbury, 2002).

**Be aware of English proficiency levels.** The size of an ELL's English vocabulary is a predictor of his proficiency in the language. Research has shown that there is a close correlation between vocabulary size/knowledge and reading/writing (Nation, 2006; Stehr, 2008; Zareva, et al., 2005). As discussed earlier, ELLs often have a significantly smaller vocabulary size than their native English-speaking students, which influences word and passage comprehension. Because textbook and dictionary definitions contain new and unfamiliar words, a limited vocabulary frustrates students who try to use these resources to learn new vocabulary words.

ESL and bilingual teachers can provide a good resource for understanding the English proficiency level for an ELL student. Besides offering insights into students' proficiency levels, ESL teachers can help design an appropriate and meaningful glossary for students. If this resource is not available, teachers can use Appendix H, which describes ELLs' English proficiency levels, as a guide to design teacher-made glossaries.

These teacher-made glossaries tailored to the needs of ELLs are important in any heterogeneous class setting composed of both native English speakers and ELLs, the norm in today's secondary classroom.

**Level the reading resources.** Many textbooks used in subject-matter classes at the secondary level are written for native English-speaking students or students whose reading levels are at their grade levels. Yet, the texts are filled with new words that are well above the English language proficiency levels of your ELLs. Obviously, alternative reading selections are required. By creatively selecting alternatives, the teacher not only provides meaningful reading for these students but also creates a meaningful context for these students to learn new vocabulary/concepts.

In addition, subject-matter teachers themselves can do some rewriting of existing textbook passages to adjust the reading to the students' level. Research has shown that reading material which provides sufficient familiar information, redundancy, and interesting writing often is an effective source for vocabulary development. Jameson (1998) and Nation (1990) discussed the general guidelines for simplifying reading passages:

- Change complex and long sentences into simple and short sentences.
- Underline key vocabulary and provide meaning on the side in parentheses.
- Remove unfamiliar words that are not essential for understanding the reading.
- Highlight the main idea of the passage with headings, summaries, or repeating key phrases.
- Use explicit, active-voice writing that is free of colloquial language or jargon.

**Ask questions.** Questions are the cornerstones of successful learning. They are also the cornerstones of successful vocabulary learning. When the teacher anchors the class discussion on a series of questions about a concept or vocabulary, vocabulary learning takes on new meaning in that students are actively thinking about the word and talking about the word, thus achieving deeper understanding of the word. Sample vocabulary-based discussion questions can begin with the teacher asking an open-ended but simple question to get students on board in the journey of meaning making. Gradually, the teacher guides the students—without giving the definition of the word—to figure out the meaning of the word itself through examining the context, comparing and contrasting possible meanings, evaluating different perspectives, and reasoning. When working with ELLs, make sure that the questions and examples you give are comprehensible to these students and background knowledge required for arriving at the correct meaning of the word is activated or taught.

## Ingredients of Effective Vocabulary Instruction

Effective vocabulary instruction requires the systematic and constant weaving of vocabulary instruction into lessons. The integrated vocabulary and subject-matter content instruction effectively means that vocabulary instruction is placed at the center of the lesson and not presented as a marginal afterthought.

Research has shown quite a few effective strategies to help a teacher weave vocabulary instruction into the lesson. You will find more about the strategies in this book.

**Effective vocabulary instruction activates prior knowledge and relates the new word to students' lives and past experiences.** Prior knowledge encompasses just about everything the student has experienced, such as native language, culture, the home country's educational systems, life experiences, immigrant experiences through their travels, and interactions with non-native English-speaking communities here. Constantly relating new words to what is already known helps students create and expand their schemata and build connections between concepts.

Chapter Two specifically explains varied strategies that help teachers activate ELLs' prior knowledge and relate new word to their lives.

**Effective vocabulary instruction focuses on conceptual subject-matter knowledge.** As discussed earlier, a teacher who successfully teaches subject-matter vocabulary closely links a new word with the concepts that the word represents (Blachowicz & Fisher, 2010; Graves, 2006, 1987). As you select and focus on the words that conceive of and express concepts and ideas, the word/concept can be:

- A new word that represents a new concept, such as *legislation* in social studies
- A new word that represents an already reviewed concept, such as *protagonist* for *main character* in English
- An old word that represents a new concept, such as *grave* for *very slow* in music
- A commonly used word that represents different concepts in different disciplines, such as *positive* for *a real number greater than zero* in mathematics or *space that is occupied* in art

Chapter Three discusses and demonstrates concept-based vocabulary instruction, including analogies, inquiry discussions, comparisons, graphic organizers, visuals, and more.

**Effective vocabulary instruction actively involves multiple senses through multiple encounters in relevant and meaningful contexts.** These interactions can be verbal or non-verbal. They can be visual, audio, kinesthetic, etc. Researchers (Graves, 2007; Marzano, 2005; Shanklin, 2007) have noted that it takes at least six meaningful exposures to learn a new word. By exposing students to new words over time in rich and relevant contexts, students learn how to tease out important aspects of word meaning and comprehend subtle differences in usage.

Chapter Four addresses these strategies and illustrates activity ideas.

**Effective vocabulary instruction should engage students in talking, thinking, and writing about the new word.** Quality vocabulary instruction moves students beyond word recognition and definition memorization. It creates opportunities for students to apply the words they learn in meaningful and authentic ways. It is only through using the words for real purposes that students will achieve a full understanding of the word and include it in their own vocabulary repertoire.

Chapter Five includes several activities that engage ELLs in writing with words they have learned. Chapters Three and Four also contain activities that involve students talking and thinking using the words learned.

**Effective vocabulary instruction should model word-learning strategies that students can apply themselves.** Formal classroom instruction in vocabulary functions as the *beginning* point of learning vocabulary, not its end (Marzano, 2005). To sustain and extend classroom vocabulary learning experiences, subject-matter teachers need to cultivate students' appreciation of language use around them, increase general word awareness, and develop and model word-learning strategies. It is only when students have become sincerely interested in language use, understood the significant impact of vocabulary on their academic learning, and developed word-learning strategies that they can become independent learners.

Many English language learners are fascinated by the generative power of the English language—the system of word formation, word combination, and variation of word meanings. Explicit instruction in generative strategies helps ELLs learn to learn on their own. After all, vocabulary acquisition, like reading and writing, is a life-long process.

The following chart contains a general guide to the principled strategies and activities presented by stages of instruction: pre-reading/teaching, initial instruction, in the middle of vocabulary instruction, and after vocabulary instruction. Please keep in mind that some of these activities can be used across instructional stages if necessary, depending on classroom contexts and goals.

### Table 2: ESL Vocabulary Teaching Strategy and Activity Overview

| Activity | Page # | Stage of instruction | Strategies |
|---|---|---|---|
| Using cognates | 12 | Pre-teaching or initial instruction | Activating prior knowledge |
| Multilingual visual glossary | 13 | Pre-teaching or initial instruction | Activating prior knowledge<br>Using multiple senses |
| Cross-cultural word-comparison web | 15 | During or after vocabulary instruction | Concept-based learning<br>Activating prior knowledge<br>Using multiple senses |
| Cross-cultural concept collage | 17 | During or after vocabulary instruction | Concept-based learning<br>Activating prior knowledge<br>Using multiple senses |
| Cross-cultural picture dictionary | 20 | During or after vocabulary instruction | Concept-based learning<br>Activating prior knowledge<br>Using multiple senses |
| Using analogies | 23 | During vocabulary instruction | Concept-based learning<br>Using multiple senses |
| Word palette | 30 | During vocabulary instruction | Concept-based learning<br>Using multiple senses |
| Word web | 32 | During vocabulary instruction | Concept-based learning<br>Using multiple senses<br>Generative word learning |
| Theme-based vocabulary | 36 | Initial encounters or during vocabulary instruction | Concept-based learning |
| Source-based vocabulary | 38 | After vocabulary instruction | Generative word learning<br>Using multiple senses<br>Teaching word learning strategies |

| Activity | Page # | Stage of instruction | Strategies |
|---|---|---|---|
| Graphic organizers | 46 | During vocabulary instruction | Concept-based learning<br>Using multiple senses |
| Word inquiry discussions | 43 | During vocabulary instruction | Inductive, meaningful, and context oriented word learning |
| Keyword method | 59 | During vocabulary instruction and after vocabulary instruction | Word learning strategies<br>Using multiple senses<br>Generative word learning |
| Word hunt | 85 | After vocabulary instruction | Word learning strategies<br>Generative word learning |
| Total physical response (TPR) | 63 | Initial or during vocabulary instruction | Using multiple senses |
| Word connotation | 68 | During vocabulary instruction | Prior knowledge<br>Deeper understanding |
| Euphemism | 72 | During vocabulary instruction or after vocabulary instruction | Deeper understanding<br>Generative word learning<br>Concept-based learning |
| Read-aloud & think-aloud | 95 | During vocabulary instruction | Word learning strategies<br>Relevant, meaningful context<br>Talking and thinking about the word |
| Word structure | 73 | During vocabulary instruction | Generative word learning<br>Word learning strategies |
| Context clues | 77 | During vocabulary instruction | Word learning strategies<br>Relevant, meaningful context |
| Vocabulary haiku | 100 | After vocabulary instruction | Using multiple senses and relating to multiple intelligences<br>Thinking and writing about the word |
| Word sensory poem | 102 | After vocabulary instruction | Using multiple senses<br>Talking, thinking, and writing about the word<br>Deeper understanding |
| Word postcard | 104 | After vocabulary instruction | Using multiple senses and relating to multiple intelligences<br>Talking, thinking, and writing about the word |
| Word buffet | 104 | After vocabulary instruction | Using multiple senses and relating to multiple intelligences<br>Talking, thinking, and writing about the word |
| Word alternatives | 109 | After vocabulary instruction | Talking, thinking, and writing about the word |
| Writer's word palette | 105 | After vocabulary instruction | Concept-based learning<br>Talking, thinking, and writing about the word |
| Math symbol translation | 109 | During vocabulary instruction | Talking, thinking, and writing about the word |

| Activity | Page # | Stage of instruction | Strategies |
|---|---|---|---|
| Word rap | 115 | After vocabulary instruction | Talking, thinking, and writing about the word |
| Word interview | 83 | After vocabulary instruction | Talking, thinking, and writing about the word<br>Word learning strategies |
| Word storytelling | 91 | After vocabulary instruction | Talking, thinking, and writing about the word<br>Word learning strategies |
| Homophones and homographs | 91 | During or after vocabulary instruction | Using multiple senses<br>Relevant and meaningful contexts<br>Generative word learning |
| Idiom posters | 87 | After vocabulary instruction | Talking, thinking, and writing about the word<br>Word learning strategies<br>Using multiple senses |

# CHAPTER 2
## Tapping into Prior Knowledge to Teach Vocabulary

• • • • •

*A rose, maybe, is a rose, but it is not une rose, is not eine Rose,*
*but multiple ways of viewing and talking about roses.*
—*Claire Kramsch*

Research has repeatedly shown that learners learn vocabulary more effectively when they can articulate what they know and make active associations between what they already know and what they are trying to learn, even if they express that prior knowledge in a language other than English.

Although many lack English language skills and specific background knowledge that subject-matter teachers expect, ELLs do bring rich prior knowledge that can be tapped into and built upon. Most have already acquired their native languages, native-language literacy skills, and subject-matter knowledge from years of school in their native countries. Some ELLs may have had more advanced learning in certain subject-matter knowledge, such as mathematics, the sciences, and history, than their native English-speaking peers. Even those with limited schooling elsewhere have acquired oral and social skills and possess cultural knowledge about their native languages.

Despite the fact that their native languages and prior knowledge may be different from or not valued highly in the American subject-matter classroom, this knowledge is still a rich, often under-utilized resource that can be tapped into when teaching vocabulary. Prior knowledge and experiences significantly influence what these students learn and how they view learning at the secondary level.

If teachers harness the power of prior knowledge and use it as an instructional tool, students will be able to make connections between what they know and the new knowledge. Vocabulary acquisition, so critical to knowledge of subject matter, becomes comprehensible, meaningful, and interesting.

In this chapter, I discuss three ways of making good use of these students' native language and prior knowledge: cross-language transfer, cross-cultural comparisons, and making ELLs' prior knowledge relevant to the class discussion topic.

# Cross-language Transfer: Cognates

Cognates are words that share the same, or similar, spelling and meaning across languages. As a second-language learner myself, I know cross-language transfers happen automatically, especially at the beginning stage of second-language acquisition, when our ability to use the new language to make meaning is limited. We look for a one-to-one correspondence in word meaning between our native language and the new language.

Even if there is no direct correspondence, we look for patterns and similarities between languages to achieve full and rapid understanding of the new language. Researchers, such as Cummins (1979), argued that ELLs' native language vocabularies influence their second-language vocabulary acquisition greatly because of linguistic and cognitive interdependences that languages can share.

This is especially true for academic vocabulary learning at the secondary level. For example, the concept of *evaporation* is the same across languages, although the word for the process differs. ELLs who have already learned this particular science concept may just need to learn how to express the concept in English.

Recent research has found a large number of cognates in academic and disciplinary-specific vocabulary between English and the Romance languages. Several research findings have also shown the effectiveness of using these cognates to learn English vocabulary among Spanish-speaking adolescents and adults.

**Side-by-side glossary.** If the subject-matter teacher is not bilingual, she can collaborate with bilingual, ESL, and foreign-language teachers to identify cognates in the reading or compile a glossary of key, discipline-specific cognates. In their multilingual classes, teachers can invite students who can speak both English and a Romance language well to help with identifying and selecting cognates. Once the cognates are identified, the teacher can either use them to modify the challenging reading or create a side-by-side glossary for those ELLs who need additional language support.

John, a native Spanish-speaking, pre-service teacher, illustrates the potential of incorporating Spanish/English cognates in the reading passage on the following page, which he modified from the science textbook on the topic of hibernation (Dong, 2009).

### Hibernation (Hibernación)

In the fall, mammals (mamíferos), such as mice and squirrels, gather and store food. Woodchucks and skunks develop thick layers of fat. These adaptations (adaptaciones), and others (otros), help many animals (animales) survive the cold winter months when food is scarce. Some birds and insects (insectos) migrate (emigran) from the forest to warmer climates (climas) where food is abundant (abundante). Small animals, such as snakes and chipmunks, spend the winter in burrows in a sleep-like state called hibernation (hibernación). During hibernation, an animal's body temperature (temperatura) is lower and its heartbeat and breathing rates decrease. Hibernation allows an animal (animal) to survive the winter on very little energy (energía). In the spring, the animal "wakes up." (29)

The Spanish-English cognates John identified and displayed in parentheses give ELLs an extra tool to help them crack the codes of the challenging academic text and achieve understanding of those daunting academic vocabulary words in English.

**Multilingual visual glossary.** Obviously, this approach doesn't work with students whose native languages do not share cognates with English. The multilingual visual glossary on the following page allows you to accomplish the same objective with native, non-Romance-language speakers.

By being aware of the positive influence of the native language (L1) on second-language (L2) vocabulary acquisition, teachers can creatively design visual glossaries on key vocabulary to be taught before a lesson.

Teachers do not have to speak another language other than English to use the multilingual glossary. Instead, they can invite their multilingual students, or bilingual or foreign-language teachers, to give L1 translations of those words. By including students' native language as a legitimate source of learning, ELLs will be more motivated and have more means to learn vocabulary. In addition, using visuals, such as pictures and drawings, can enhance comprehension. Finally, comparing words between different languages can lead to higher levels of thinking about the concept and promote student confidence and engagement.

Note that in designing a multilingual glossary, care should be taken to avoid using difficult words to define new words. Regular English dictionary definitions are not a good choice for selecting definitions. (See the Suggested Resources in the back of this book for websites providing free translations and for names of two good dictionaries to use with ELLs.)

Following is an example of a multilingual visual glossary developed by Vincent, a mathematics pre-service teacher, and his ELLs (Dong, 2009). This multilingual geometry picture glossary was used to teach the angle bisector theorem (Figure 1).

**Figure 1: Multilingual Picture Geometry Glossary**

Angle Bisector Theorem: If two sides of a triangle are congruent, then the angles opposite these sides are congruent.

| English | Spanish | French | Portuguese | Chinese | Korean |
|---|---|---|---|---|---|
| Triangle  | triángulo | triangle | triângulo | might | 삼각형 |
| Vertex 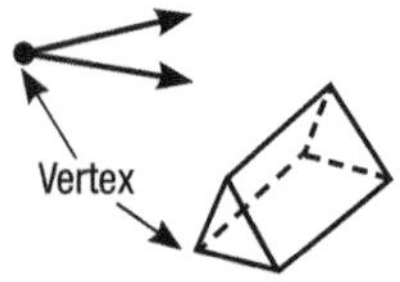 | Vértice | Sommet | Vértice | 顶点 | 꼭지점 |
| Angle bisector 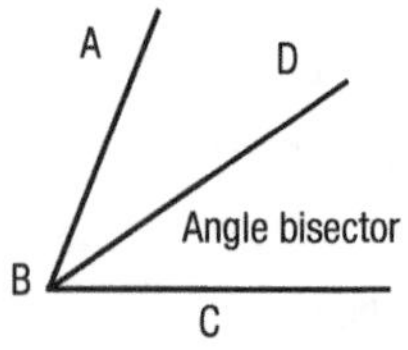 | Bisector de anglo | Ligne de bissection de montage | Bissetor de ângulo | 角平分线 | 각도를 이등분 |
| Congruent sides (≅) 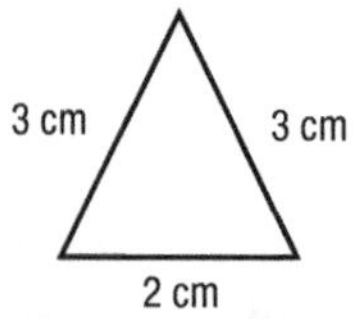 | lados congruente | côtés congruent | lados congruente | 等边 | 합동 측면 |
| Congruent angles (≅) 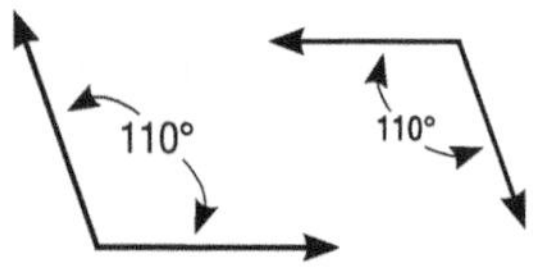 | ángulos congruentes | angles congruents | ângulos congruentes | 等角 | 합동 각도 |
| Isosceles triangle 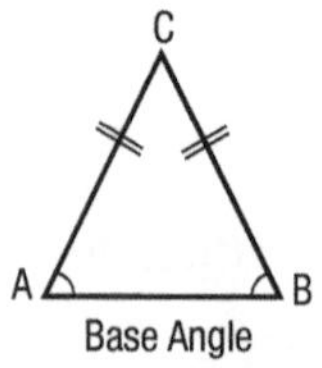 | triángulo isósceles | triangle isocèle | triângulo isósceles | 等腰三角形 | 이등변 삼각형 |
| Theorem: a statement which has been proved to be true. | Teorema | Théorème | Teorema | 定理 | 정리 |

# Cross-cultural Comparisons

Jean, a biology pre-service teacher, was tutoring the concept of biomes to three ELLs. She prepared a glossary and map; however, she still felt unsure about whether her students could understand the concept of biomes. After consulting with the ESL teacher, Jean designed a worksheet using her students' backgrounds as an entry point into the lesson.

During the lesson, she and the students discussed their home countries and the biome concept. Once she sensed the students had a good grasp of the concept, Jean asked them to write about the type of biome in their home country and compare it with a biome in the U.S. Students had fun with the activity. In doing so, they related the new knowledge with something they knew, thus gaining a good understanding of the concept of biomes. Below is an example of their writing.

**Table 3: Cross-cultural Biome Comparisons**

### Cross-cultural Biome Comparisons

| Geographic location | My country: Ecuador | New York |
|---|---|---|
| Types of biomes | Tropical rainforest | Temperate forest |
| Weather | It is always hot and humid year round, and it rains a lot. It has 6-30 feet of rain in a year. | It is warm in summer, but cold in winter. It has about 5-16 feet of rain in a year. |
| Temperature | Average 65° or above for the year | Average 20°-60° for the year |
| Plants | Plantain trees, palm trees, mango trees, and orange trees | Shrubs and deciduous trees, such as maple trees, walnut trees, birch trees, dogwoods, willow trees, fir, etc. |
| Animals | Vultures, crabs, cats, mice, snakes, monkeys, mosquitoes, fish, shrimps, dogs, dragon flies, horses, cows | Deer, owls, squirrels, bears, rabbits, skunks, raccoons, hummingbirds, eagles, etc. |

### Biome Comparisons

| Biome: The total amount of living things in a region, such as a rainforest. | |
|---|---|
| Comparing the two biomes | Both temperate and tropical rainforests have wet and hot days in a year. They both have a lot of plants, animals, and food chains. But here in New York City, we have more cold and dry days in a year. I'm not used to it yet. I still like to live in a tropical rainforest like my country where I can eat all sorts of tropical fruits and climb the palm tree. |

**Cross-cultural concept-comparison webs.** Cross-cultural concept comparisons require the teacher to engage the class by using what ELLs know from their native language to compare and contrast key concepts under study. The teacher can select the concept from either the reading or class discussion and focus on it for a sustained amount of time for deeper understanding.

The concept can be put on the board as the focal point of a word web for exploration. ELLs are welcomed to offer their understanding of the concept in their native language. For example, the concept of propaganda can be discussed simply by writing the word on the board, drawing a circle around it, and asking students to offer relevant, related words that create a web. After webbing, the teacher can engage the class to group the synonyms or related words into categories and further the discussion of the concept in terms of its connotation and context in use (Figure 2).

**Figure 2: Venn Diagram of *Propaganda***

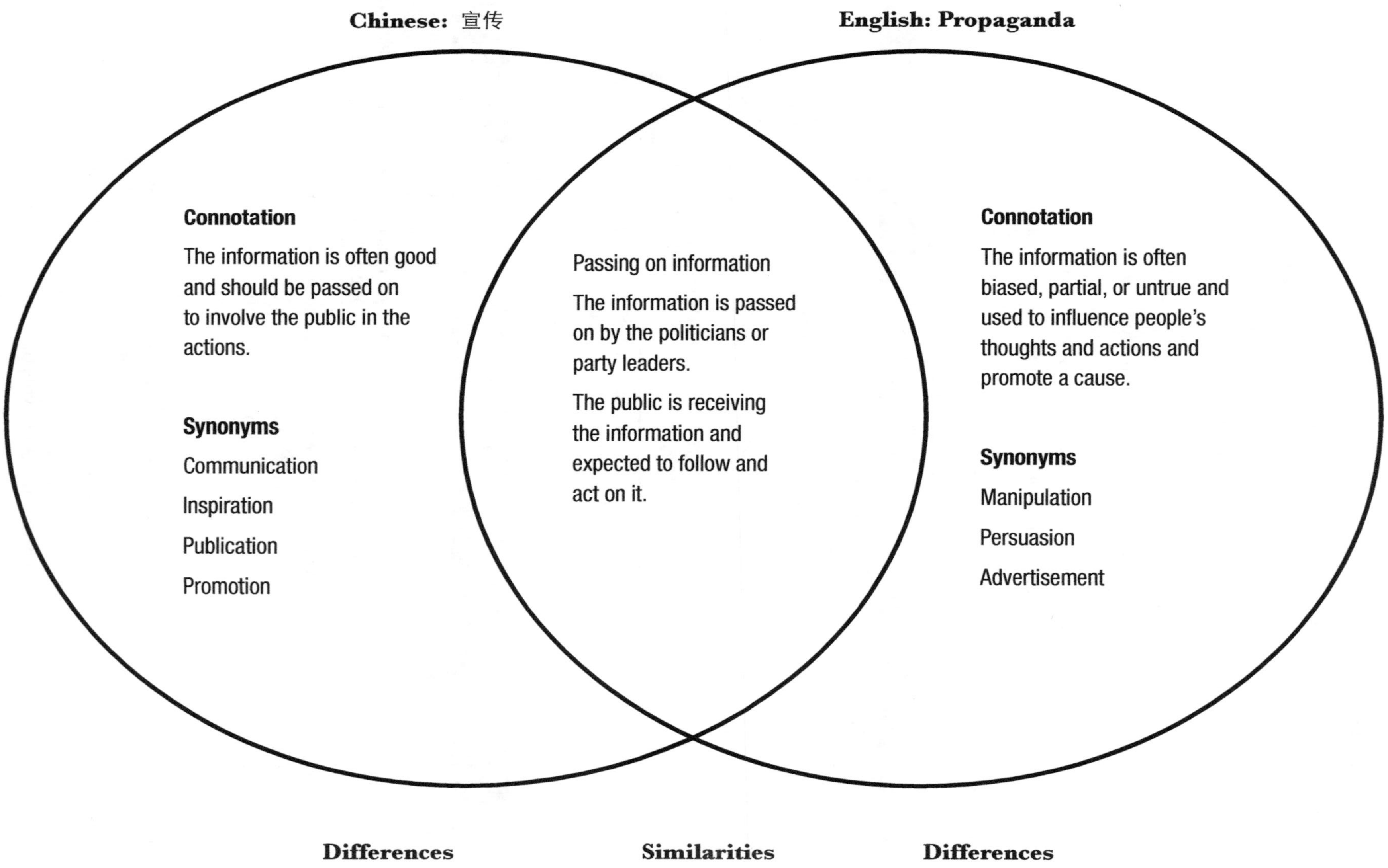

**Chinese:** 宣传

**English: Propaganda**

**Connotation**

The information is often good and should be passed on to involve the public in the actions.

**Synonyms**

Communication

Inspiration

Publication

Promotion

Passing on information

The information is passed on by the politicians or party leaders.

The public is receiving the information and expected to follow and act on it.

**Connotation**

The information is often biased, partial, or untrue and used to influence people's thoughts and actions and promote a cause.

**Synonyms**

Manipulation

Persuasion

Advertisement

**Differences**

**Similarities**

**Differences**

Concept-comparison webs are useful because word concepts often vary from culture to culture and from language to language in meaning and connotation. A side-by-side comparison of these variations can lead to a deeper understanding and critical discussion of the word. For example, based on American cultural practices and values, argument is a healthy and welcomed activity and is viewed with largely positive connotations—lawyers arguing their cases, students writing argumentative essays, and politicians arguing their positions on the issues.

In other cultures, however, argument is not viewed in a positive light. In Chinese culture, for example, argument is viewed as negatively detrimental to social harmony and something that should be avoided at all times. In contrast, English contains quite a few metaphorical expressions about the word *argument* that depicts it like a game or a battle of wits. Chinese students need to learn the concepts behind and the expressions about the word *argument* in order for them to understand the significance of arguments in American culture and to be able to participate fully in U.S. society. A side-by-side comparison on expressions used to describe the concept of argument in America and China illustrates this point (Dong, 2004, p. 31):

**Cross-cultural Concept Comparison: Argument in America and in China**

| **Argument in America** | **Argument in China** |
|---|---|
| Your claims are indefensible. | Truth is in the open, and you don't need to argue. |
| He attacked every weak point in my argument. | Because of his wrongdoing, he has to argue his way out. |
| Her criticism was right on target. | No matter how good your argument is, away from the truth is not right. |
| I've never won an argument against him. | Due to lack of intelligence, he has to use argument. |
| He shot down all of my arguments. | You should give in to the argument to maintain harmony. |

Comparing vocabulary use across languages like this helps second-language students learn and understand the underlying concepts behind a new vocabulary word. In addition, the comparison reveals differences in attitudes stemming from differences in cultural beliefs and values. ELLs can use such comparisons to gain cultural insights and understand why American culture and American classrooms do the things they do. Once a conceptual understanding is achieved, these students will be able to use words such as *argument* with confidence and meaning.

**Cross-cultural concept collages.** Speakers of different languages have different emotional and conceptual associations for color-related words. In reading *Good Earth* by Pearl Buck, Amy, an English teacher, invited her tenth-grade class of both native and non-native English-speaking students to design collages that centered around a specific color described in the book, such as red, white, and yellow. Students worked in groups of three to five to design their word collages with specific goals in mind:

- Cite from the literature to highlight a specific color and its significance.
- Create some visuals by drawing or downloading online pictures to describe the symbolic use of this color.
- Compare and contrast the meaning of this color between the Chinese culture and American culture.

Following is an example of such a collage (Figure 3).

**Figure 3: Cross-cultural Concept Collage 1**

In reading *The Joy Luck Club* by Amy Tan, the concept of shame came up repeatedly in the book and class discussion. Alex, an English teacher of a diverse eleventh-grade class with both ELLs and non-ELLs, considered the shame concept as critical in students' understanding of several stories, thus worthy of an in-depth study. Tapping into his students' prior knowledge, he assigned his class to do a shame concept investigation. Students were encouraged to go online and interview their parents about the shame concept and its cultural significance in both Chinese culture and American culture. Students then came up with a group collage like this (Figure 4).

**Figure 4: Cross-cultural Concept Collage 2**

**Textual support**

p. 99, "Rules of the Game":

When Waverly Jong walked home with her mother, her mother kept bragging about her talent for chess. Waverly felt ashamed. Her mother asked, "So shame be with mother?" Waverly says, "Just embarrassing." "Embarrassed you be my daughter?" her mother asks.

We interpret Waverly's shame as the American shame meaning embarrassed.

p. 36, "Scar":

An-Mei was told by her Popo that her mother committed a shameful act by marrying another man and becoming his fourth wife after her first husband died.

We interpret the shame Popo talked about as the Chinese shame, disgrace, dishonor—far more serious than the American shame.

**Usages**

It's a shame.

What a shame!

Shame on you.

Crying shame.

You ought to be ashamed of yourself.

Fool me once, shame on you; fool me twice, shame on me.

**American shame**

An embarrassment or feelings of guilt; e.g., David Letterman, Eliot Spitzer

The meaning is narrower. And the shameful feeling is not as long lasting as Chinese shame. It's more like a bump in the road, and there is a second chance.

**Chinese shame**

Failing family responsibilities; honoring traditions, parents, elders, and authorities

The social and cultural impact of shameful feelings lasts longer and has far-reaching influence on a person's social being, reputation, and public acceptance.

**Cross-cultural proverb picture dictionary.** In Pictionary, players try to guess a word from a fellow player's drawing. Cross-cultural proverb picture dictionary requires students to work as a team to draw not only an English proverb but also proverbs in other languages that share similar meanings with their English counterparts. This activity helps ELLs visualize the words and facilitate conceptual understanding and language appreciation.

In doing so, students make active associations between pictures and words and between symbols and cultural values. ELLs enjoy an equal playing field with their native English-speaking peers as they demonstrate their knowledge of their native language and, in the process, perhaps teach the class a thing or two.

Proverbs are metaphorical in nature. By tackling them from the visual perspective first, the teacher can engage the class to not only remember the metaphorical meaning but also initiate comparative discussions on cultural similarities and differences in a more concrete and creative manner. Over time, both students and the teacher can collect proverbs all over the world and categorize them according to shared metaphorical meanings and contexts where they are used.

The following is a list of such proverbs and a sample picture dictionary (Figure 5).

> The early bird catches the worm. (English)
> God helps those who rise early. (Spanish, Russian, French)
> The buffaloes that come late will drink bad water. (Vietnamese)
> Clumsy birds have need of early flight. (Chinese)
> If diligent, even a beggar can get warm rice. (Korean)

**Figure 5: Cross-cultural Proverb Picture Dictionary**

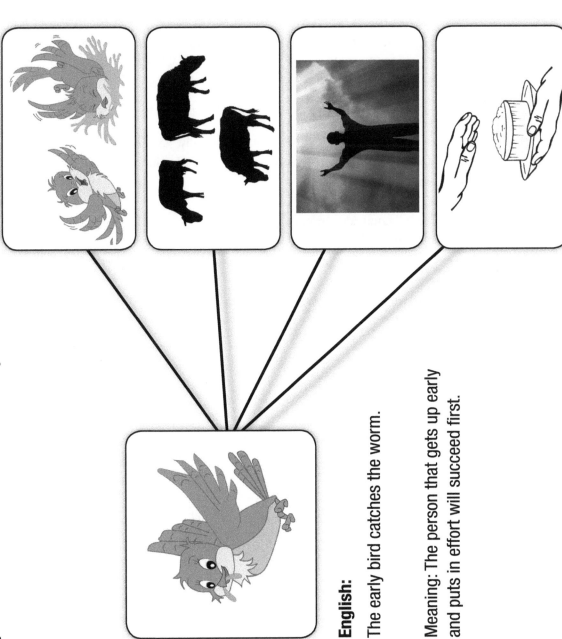

**Chinese:**
Clumsy birds have need of early flight.

**Vietnamese:**
The buffaloes that come late will drink bad water.

**Spanish/Russian/French:**
God helps those who rise early.

**Korean:**
If diligent, even a beggar can get warm rice.

**English:**
The early bird catches the worm.

Meaning: The person that gets up early and puts in effort will succeed first.

# Making ELLs' Prior Knowledge Relevant to the Class Discussion Topic

Subject-matter teachers should remember that ELLs may have limited English, but they are still capable of thinking critically. As long as the teacher purposefully taps into the students' prior knowledge and makes the class discussion topic relevant, these students will respond with enthusiasm and intelligence.

For example, using literature that is closely related to ELLs' experience and background and discussing concepts like immigration and education motivates and engages these students and allows them to share their perspective and insights with the rest of the class. Often, native English-speaking students do not have insight or critical perspective towards these issues due to lack of experience. ELLs who have gone through immigration and ESL/bilingual instruction, however, can provide an ideal context for in-depth vocabulary learning in this area.

Marian, an English teacher, utilized this prior knowledge to teach the concept of bilingual education to her mainstream tenth-grade class while they read *When I Was Puerto Rican*, by Esmeralda Santiago. Discussion focused on Negi's reaction to being thrown into an English-speaking mainstream class to learn English.

During the discussion on bilingual education, Marian purposefully gave her ELLs the opportunity to voice their opinions and reactions as they compared bilingual education and instruction using English as a second language (Dong, 2004).

> Teacher: I believe bilingual education is appropriate.
> Karen: I remember when I came to the U.S., I was put into a bilingual class and there were Chinese kids in there who had to listen to Spanish and English instruction. They were never taught in Chinese.
> Jessica: If Negi takes bilingual classes, she'll learn at her level and she'll learn both languages. She'll have more of an advantage because if they put her in an all-English class, she won't know anything.
> Joel: They should put kids in an all-English class.
> Teacher: Why?
> Joel: Because when I came to this country, they put me into an all-English class. But they put my brother into a bilingual class. I learned English within about three months. He still doesn't know very much English. [Reaction from other students: "Wow."]
> Evelyn: But if you put a kid that doesn't know English into an all-English class, he'll just sit there lost.
> Vicky: But if he sits there quiet, he can observe and learn.
> Adam: Couldn't they have a separate place to learn English?
> Jonathan: Yeah-it's called school! [laughter]
> Vicky: How would feel if you were Negi?
> Jessica: Uncomfortable. It would be so hard.

As this class discussion excerpt illustrates, activating prior knowledge to teach vocabulary creates a rich context for learning. Complex and abstract vocabulary becomes comprehensible and meaningful.

# CHAPTER 3
## Concept-based Vocabulary Instruction

· · · · ·

*Language shapes the way we think, and determines what we can think about.*
—*Benjamin Lee Whorf*

Secondary teachers teach concepts and ideas every day. These concepts and ideas are introduced to clarify and further students' thinking, to enable them to express themselves, and to understand and apply content knowledge. As discussed in the introduction, vocabulary learning at the secondary level is concept learning. The concepts and ideas are verbalized and expressed in words.

Vocabulary instruction that focuses on concepts performs a double duty—teaching both subject-matter and vocabulary knowledge. Concept-based vocabulary instruction enables students to gain an in-depth understanding of the semantics of the words and relationships between words that represent and express ideas and concepts. Teaching vocabulary in this way involves linking individual words with larger concepts under study, associating new words with familiar concepts (as seen in the previous chapter), visualizing word relationships and organizational patterns, and explicitly teaching metaphorical meanings.

## Using Analogies to Teach Vocabulary

Analogies use comparisons of similar and familiar concepts to help students understand new concepts. We all have experienced the "Aha!" moment when someone made a difficult concept understandable through an analogy. Using an analogy is an effective way to engage students in relating what they know to what they do not know in order to understand an abstract or complex vocabulary concept.

Analogies have been used widely and are proven effective across all subjects to motivate students, clarify thinking, and crystallize difficult concepts. In teaching academic and discipline-specific vocabulary, teachers should always look for good analogies to explain abstract and difficult concepts.

When using analogies to teach vocabulary to ELLs, teachers should be aware of possible differences in thought processes in different cultures. According to the Whorfian Hypothesis, words shape our thinking. For example, the fact that Eskimos have many different words to describe snow reveals that their view toward snow is different than Americans' view of snow. Their analogy of snow is probably different from that of Americans as well. Teachers need to re-examine the analogies they use for comprehension, relevance, and understanding when using them with ELLs. Teachers also need to be open to any analogies that come from ELLs' native cultures even though they may be expressed in another language and may be foreign to the teacher and native English-speaking students.

Tailoring analogies to this group of students builds upon these students' prior knowledge and ensures that the new concept will be understood. In a way, thinking about, or re-examining, language and basic concepts like this is a lot like thinking backwards.

Sally, a biology teacher, often reminds herself to think backwards when teaching ELL students biological vocabulary and concepts. "You cannot assume students know basic words that are used to describe the concepts," she says. This "backward" thinking or re-examining the language and even prototypes used to teach biological concepts leads Sally to be reflective and thorough in her lesson planning (Dong, 2002, p. 45):

> You can see, for example, the crayfish for students who may never see crayfish or know crayfish. If a textbook never supplements the picture of crayfish, I, the teacher have to first define a crayfish: What does it look like? What's the color? So there are certain things that we take for granted. For example, we would say a blue jay and a sparrow, like common things that children would see on the curb when they grow up here. But for these children, they may never see these things before since they are new to this country. So you really have to think backwards. If the child never saw the item, let alone the internal structure before, the first thing you have to introduce is what it is and how it is, and then you can teach biology.

In her efforts to make the new concepts comprehensible and accessible to her students, Sally used modified or elaborated definitions of the new words, physical movements to create a mental picture of the meaning, and examples and analogies from students' daily lives to provide the contexts for students' scientific knowledge building. The following is an example of these techniques at work (Dong, 2002, p. 45):

> Teacher: Number ten is a large vacuole (wrote on the board). A vacuole stores the water and other substances for the cell. The vacuole in the animal cell is tiny because the animal can go and get water, right? But the trees cannot grow legs. So it has to absorb the water and holds the water in the cell to hold on to it (used gestures and physical movements).
>
> Student: Like camels—they hold up their water.
>
> Teacher: You got it—same idea.

Here Sally paints a clear mental picture of the word *vacuole* by using simple language, physical movements, and a humorous comparison between an animal cell and a plant cell to scaffold ELL students' learning. Instead of giving definitions, Sally pushes students to come up with analogies they are familiar with—in this case, a camel—to describe the function of a plant vacuole.

**Analogy pools.** Students relate well to analogies, which build conceptual bridges that get the meaning across, especially when those concepts are abstract and complex. Teachers can plan the vocabulary by associating the abstract concept with something concrete that students know. Below is Glynn's example of a series of analogies on animal cells with pictures (Figure 6: Paris & Glynn, 2004):

| **The factory** | **Animal cell** |
|---|---|
| security guard | plasma membrane |
| control center | nucleus |
| power generator | mitochondria |
| production machines | ribosome |
| inside hallways | endoplasmic reticulum |

**Figure 6: Cell and City Analogy Visualization**

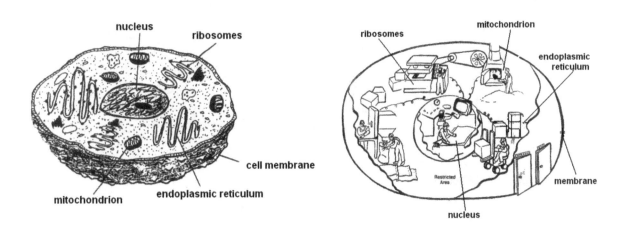

(From *Contemporary Educational Psychology, 29* (3) (2004), 230-247 in an article written by Nita A. Paris and Shawn M. Glynn, "Elaborate analogies in science text: Tools for enhancing preservice teachers' knowledge and attitudes." © (2004) by Elsevier.)

Robert, a ninth-grade biology teacher, took into consideration that some of the analogy examples may be foreign to ELLs to begin with. Therefore, he tried to use examples that his ELLs could relate and understand. For instance, he asked his students to work in groups to generate cell analogies using the analogy that everyone knew, such as the cell and school analogy (Figure 7).

**Figure 7: Cell and School Analogy Visualization**

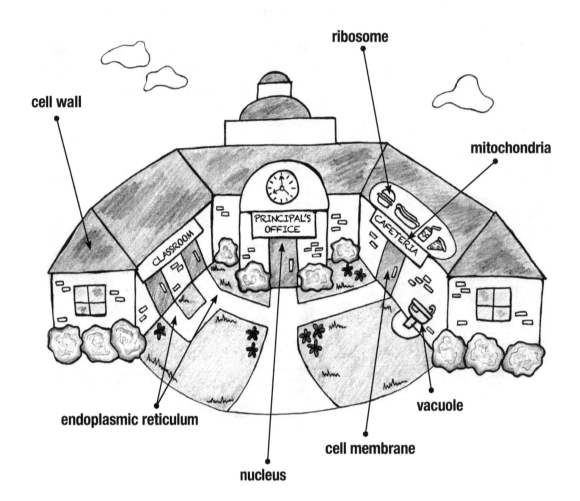

Afterward, Robert asked the class to write about their analogies and specify how the analogy helped them understand the cell concept as shown in the students' writing below.

- Cell wall: school building
- Cell membrane: the doors and walls of the classroom. Like the doors and walls of the classroom, the cell membrane contains and controls what is coming in and going out of the cell.
- Nucleus: principal. Like the principal, the nucleus is the control center of the cell.
- Mitochondria: cafeteria. Like the cafeteria providing students with food, mitochondria are the powerhouse that provides energy to the cell.
- Endoplasmic reticulum: hallways. Like students forming a line to walk between classes in the hallways, the ER forms channels and moves substances to all parts of the cell.
- Ribosome: food students get in the cafeteria. Like food to energize students, ribosome attaches to the ER and helps it make protein, which is used by the cell to grow and move more effectively.
- Vacuole: water fountains. Like a water fountain, the vacuole has an ample supply of fluid/water.

Non-science subject-matter teachers can also develop their own analogy pools to facilitate an understanding of critical concepts. For example, Chris Beers-Arthur and Brent Cook have developed a series of powerful analogies in teaching U.S. government to a class of ELLs. A social studies teacher can adapt her work to teach complex and abstract concepts as seen on the following page (Figure 8):

**Figure 8: U.S. Government Analogies**

| U.S. government | Human body |
| --- | --- |
| The judicial branch/the Supreme Court | Uncle Sam's heart |
| Legislative branch/two houses | Uncle Sam's arms |
| Executive branch/president's cabinet: | Uncle Sam's brain |
| Economic system | Uncle Sam's digestive system |
| Two main political parties | Uncle Sam's legs |

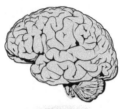

Uncle Sam's brain: executive branch: president, vice president, and cabinet

Uncle Sam's left arm: legislative branch: Senate

Uncle Sam's right arm: legislative branch: House of Representatives

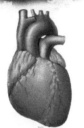

Uncle Sam's heart: judicial branch: Supreme Court

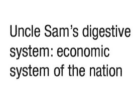

Uncle Sam's digestive system: economic system of the nation

Uncle Sam's legs: two major parties: Democratic Party and Republican Party

Once an analogy is selected and taught, the teacher should ask students to elaborate on the similarities and differences between the two concepts. ELLs can get started with sentences like *… is like … because …* or *The two share something in common in that* …. In addition, drawings or pictures should be used and labeled accordingly to reinforce the mental images. Students should be encouraged to generate their own analogies in vocabulary lessons and to write about their analogies using rubrics like these (adapted from Orgill and Thomas, 2007).

> What is your analogy?
> What are the similarities between your analogy and the new word?
> How did you come up with this analogy?
> Why does this analogy help you understand the new word?
> Draw a picture of your analogy to show the relationship between the new word and the analogy.

## Teaching Metaphorical Language

*Metaphor is pervasive in everyday life, not just in language but in thought and action. Our ordinary conceptual system, in terms of which we both think and act, is fundamentally metaphorical in nature.*
—*George Lakoff and Mark Johnson*

Metaphorical language uses one thing to express something else that either shares or does not share a similarity. According to Lakoff and Johnson (1980), metaphors are not only central to the language but also fundamental to the thought patterns of a specific culture. In secondary schools, it is through metaphorical thinking that students build conceptual knowledge to reflect and to think with abstraction.

Metaphorical language and multiple meanings of words are seldom taught in the beginning stage of second-language acquisition for fear of overwhelming L2 students with the complexities and intricacies of the language. Thus, ELLs acquire one meaning of a word, often associating the meaning with concrete sensory referents, without knowing about other meanings or metaphorical referents. Because metaphor and multiple word meanings are integral to many subject-matter classes, it is important to teach them explicitly.

As a matter of fact, learning metaphorical language is an integral part of secondary curriculum, instruction, and evaluation. An examination of the New York Regents Exams in English, social studies, and sciences shows an important share of metaphorical language. Students are required to think metaphorically and have a good grasp of conceptual metaphors that are fundamental to American culture.

For example, like many other state assessments, the New York Regents exam on U.S. government includes political cartoons like this (Figure 9):

**Figure 9: Interpreting Political Cartoons**

The main obstacle to solving the problem shown in the cartoon was the

1) Failure of Congress to respond to public opinion
2) Government's inability to fund social programs
3) Inefficiency of the government's tax collection
4) Demands of a variety of special interest groups

(From www.nysedregents.org)

In order to answer test questions, students need to recognize that the arm holding out a mug represents Uncle Sam, the U.S. government. The dollar sign on the mug signifies money—meaning Uncle Sam is asking people for money—which refers to collecting taxes from the people.

Educated in U.S. schools and immersed in American popular culture for all their lives, native English-speaking students understand the symbolic meanings, culturally relevant concepts, and metaphorical language behind all this. Thus, they are likely to be able to use their prior knowledge and conceptual framework to comprehend these metaphors in the reading and on the test.

But ELLs have not had the benefit of prior knowledge and cultural immersion to understand American metaphors. Their English vocabulary is still limited to basic and concrete words. Their time spent on learning English is too short and basic to provide them with opportunities to learn and use American-centric symbolic meanings and culturally relevant concepts.

This places demands on subject-matter teachers to teach metaphorical language explicitly to help students develop metaphorical language competence. Explicit teaching of metaphorical language requires the teacher to carefully select materials that are rich in metaphorical language, clearly link literal and metaphorical language, and highlight the cultural history and beliefs embedded in the metaphorical language.

**Word palettes and word webs.** For example, Mary, a ninth-grade English teacher, wanted to emphasize the concept of the American dream while the class studied Langston Hughes' poem "Harlem." An informal survey before the lesson helped her realize that her ELL students may not have grasped the figurative meaning of the word *dream*, let alone the American dream—even though the pursuit of a better life was the reason many of them immigrated to America. That realization prompted Mary to withhold her usual interpretive and analytical analysis of the poem and instead focus first on comprehending the concept of a dream.

Grouping her regular students with ELL students, Mary asked each group to construct a word palette of the word *dream*. A word palette is composed of the pictures of both the literal and figurative meanings of the word, as well as definitions of the word with student-composed sentences based on their understanding. The following shows how one group understood the double meaning of *dream* (Figure 10).

**Figure 10: Double Meanings of a Dream**

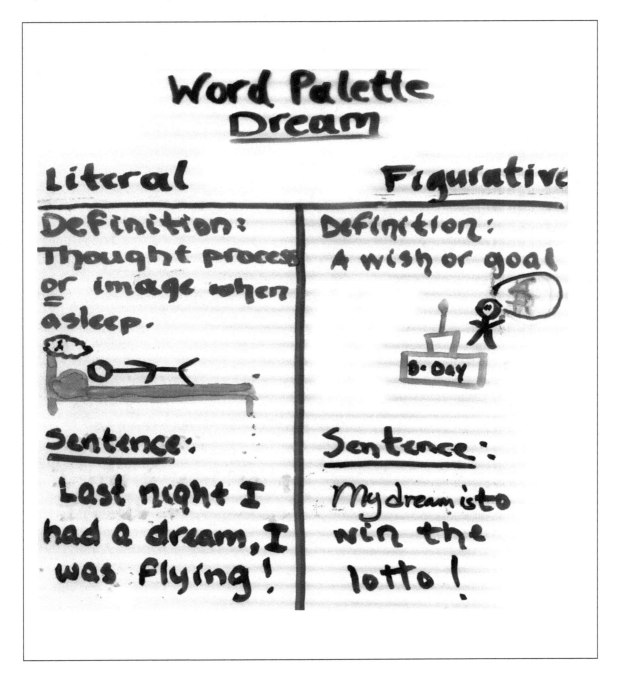

Once students achieved a metaphorical understanding of the concept of a dream, Mary then asked each student to write about their dreams. For ELLs especially, she asked them to write about what made them come to the U.S. After students shared, Mary introduced the concept of the American dream by inviting the group to compose a word web. Here is an example (Figure 11).

**Figure 11: Word Web of the American Dream**

### What is the American dream?

Based on the exploration of the dream metaphor, Mary then asked her students to work in groups to demonstrate each line of Hughes' poem by drawing a picture and linking literal and metaphorical meanings. Below are examples of these students' drawings (Figures 12, 13, 14, and 15).

**Figures 12-15: Hughes' Deferred Dream Drawings 1-4**

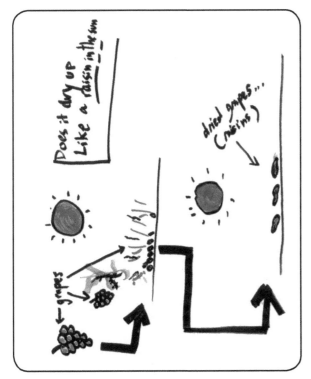

**Idiom study.** ELLs are fascinated by, but often struggle with, English idiomatic expressions like *burn the candle at both ends, a kick in the pants,* and *head over heels.* As teenagers in middle and high schools, they are eager to make sense of the complex vocabulary of conventional metaphors uttered around them both in and outside of the classroom.

Subject-matter teachers use idioms regularly and often do not pause to explain what they mean; instead, they may not even realize they are using an expression, or they may assume students already are familiar with them. Teachers should monitor their use of idiomatic expressions, and pause to make sure that ELLs understand expressions like *You are missing the boat* or *There's more to that than meets the eye.* To capitalize on the keen interest that ELLs often show for learning the expressions of American culture, teachers can also design lessons that teach conventional metaphors in a playful and meaningful way.

For instance, ELLs can work with their native English-speaking peers to generate as many idiomatic expressions as possible on a given topic. Following is an example of idiomatic expressions related to the human body (Figure 16).

**Figure 16: Idiomatic Expressions Related to the Human Body**

# Theme-based Vocabulary Instruction Promotes Concept Learning

Normally, teachers teach new words when they appear in the reading or in the lesson. These words are often not interconnected or organized around a theme, thus making vocabulary learning especially difficult for new language learners. Unlike their native English-speaking peers who already have a previous conceptual framework or vocabulary repertoire to build on, ELLs take a longer time and require multiple exposures to learn and see conceptual connections among these words. Theme-based vocabulary instruction creates a conceptual learning environment that facilitates language and concept learning at the same time.

Themes are central ideas or messages about life, society, and human nature. They can also be a subject-matter topic. In many cases, subject-matter curricula are organized by themes, such as self and society, love, ecology, theorem, etc. A theme-based curriculum gives focus and coherence to the curriculum and promotes concept learning; in fact, a curriculum often lends itself nicely to theme-based vocabulary instruction.

A theme-based teaching approach has a long history and research-proven benefits. It provides students with exposure to, and multiple methods to access, words that express the theme in various ways. Rather than randomly selecting unrelated words to learn or learning words as they occur in reading, theme-based vocabulary teaching reinforces the central idea or message conveyed in the reading. By sustaining the focus of the theme for a period of time, students will have repeated exposures to varied readings, discussions, and words used to express the theme, thus increasing understanding and word retention.

The theme-based teaching approach is a familiar organizational structure for middle school. Wiggins and Wiggins (1997) discussed the layout of such a curriculum and the potential of using a single theme to integrate all curricula, thus facilitating students' language and subject matter-concept development. In high schools, teachers can use the theme-based approach in a block schedule arrangement—such as a combined 90-minute class of English and social studies or science and math—to organize the reading and vocabulary instruction around a theme.

For example, in teaching the Holocaust unit in social studies and English, the themes of genocide, anti-Semitism, faith, father-son bonds, and tradition can be explored thoroughly and meaningfully when both classes talk about vocabulary around these themes. If coordination among disciplines is not available, teachers can still use a theme to anchor vocabulary to a concept to teach. In teaching *The Great Gatsby*, for example, the themes of the American dream, love, social class, and loyalty become anchors for vocabulary study. Students can be asked to search for words used by the characters to talk about these themes and to compare and contrast how people view themes like the American dream during the 1920s and now.

Using themes to teach vocabulary holds special appeal to ELLs because it makes word acquisition more meaningful, interconnected, and manageable. It also achieves the objectives of learning language and concepts simultaneously.

**Developing metaphors around a theme.** After selecting a theme, the teacher gathers related vocabulary from the reading and from everyday language. The teacher also can introduce a theme by either engaging the class in brainstorming the words or phrases associated with the theme or after discussing a pre-selected theme concept with the class.

Once the concept is introduced, the teacher should provide rich vocabulary, especially metaphorical language, to explore the concept and illustrate diverse ways that the theme is expressed. For example, the theme of love in Shakespeare's *A Midsummer Night's Dream* ("The course of true love never did run smooth") can be explored further by inviting students to generate as many love-related expressions similar to Shakespeare's poetic phrase as they can.

After writing these expressions on the board or overhead, the teacher can ask the class to think about the theme again. This time students should try to arrive at a metaphorical way of thinking about love, such as *Love is a journey.* By examining the language used to express that theme, students will see the bigger picture and how language shapes the way people talk about love. Even Shakespeare's poetic metaphor is derived from that same conceptualization of love. ELLs should be encouraged to share the love metaphors used in their languages.

Some examples:

> **Theme: Love is a journey.**
> We are at a crossroads.
> We'll just have to go our separate ways.
> We can't turn back now.
> I don't think this relationship is going anywhere.
> We're stuck.
> It's been a long, bumpy road.
> This relationship is a dead-end street.
> Our marriage is on the rocks.
> We've gotten off the track. (Lakoff, 1993; p. 06)

**Exploring concepts through visuals.** As mentioned earlier, the theme of propaganda is worth focusing on. This is especially true if ELLs have a different conceptualization about it in their native languages. That difference begs for the concept to be explored deeply rather than brushed off quickly. Phil teaches a class of eighth graders composed of both native English speakers and ELLs. He has paired with the social studies teacher to teach the concept of propaganda in WWII while his class reads George Orwell's *Animal Farm.*

Phil conducted an initial survey of his students' understanding of the concept of propaganda and found that many students confused the concepts of propaganda and advertisement. Even though students could substitute the equivalent term for propaganda in their native languages, Phil sensed that the meaning was lost in translation. Well aware that his students were bombarded with media messages every day, Phil decided to use something that everyone could relate to teach the word— Internet pictures depicting the nation's war against terrorism.

He showed the class a series of pictures and asked them to work in pairs to examine the picture carefully and respond to the following questions:

What is going on in the picture?
Is this a propaganda picture? Why?
What stands out the most for you? Is the image appealing to you? How so?
What is the writer or artist trying to achieve?
What ideas are being promoted?
What audience is this image geared toward? How do you know?
What strategies does the writer/artist use to communicate those ideas? Are they convincing? Why?
How is propaganda used in this picture?
How has it changed your view?

## Source-based Vocabulary Instruction

Source-based vocabulary instruction begins by teaching the meaning of one basic word, then branching out to explore the different meanings that word takes on when used with other words. It is different from theme-based vocabulary instruction in that it can start with any word, not necessarily a key concept or unifying topic under study.

Source-based vocabulary instruction is a fun way to show students how words are interrelated and build upon each other, and it helps them to understand the evolving nature of language. Research has shown that this vocabulary instructional method effectively creates a focused vocabulary-learning environment and stimulates student curiosity about language (Dong, 2004; Nilsen & Nilsen, 2003, 2004).

Because source-based vocabulary instruction emphasizes word connections and forges word relationships, it creates a meaningful and systematic way to learn vocabulary and expand students' word knowledge. Students often find the word connections fascinating, and they become very interested in exploring word use and word relationships to unravel the meaning of unknown words.

For example, the word *bread* as a typical daily food can be explored and studied not only for variations in meaning, but also for its cultural significance and contexts of its use (Dong, 2004).

Give us this day our daily bread.
My landlord wants his bread now.
Man cannot live by bread alone.
His curve ball is his bread–and–butter pitch.
This is the bread of life.
He knows which side his bread is buttered on.
Cast your bread upon water.
His invention will take bread out of many mouths.
We found him standing in a bread line.
Please stay and break bread with us. (Dong, 29)

---

Using a basic word, such as *bread*, as the starting point and then branching out to its multiple extensions in meaning provides a manageable and exciting way to learn vocabulary.

Source-based vocabulary exposes ELLs to commonly used American metaphors. With source-based vocabulary instruction, students are invited not only to intelligently guess the meaning of a word but also to discuss how these words are valued and used in American culture in social, historical, religious, and cultural contexts.

All languages share similar generative abilities, extended features in meanings, and uses based on key basic concepts and words. Source-based instruction offers a welcome opportunity for ELLs to share insights from their native languages to enlighten both the teacher and other students. For example, Chinese students can talk about the word *rice* and its extended metaphorical meanings and uses when the word is grouped with others like this:

> Rice bowl (basic necessities of life)
>
> Steel rice bowl (job safety)
>
> See sky, eat rice (counting on Mother Nature for a harvest).
>
> One mouse dropping ruins the whole pot of rice porridge (one bad apple can spoil the whole bunch).
>
> The best wife cannot cook without rice (no matter how good a chef is, she cannot cook a good meal without key ingredients to work with).
>
> Talk does not cook rice (actions speak louder than words).

Source-based vocabulary instruction is suitable for English class and for all other content-area classrooms. Teachers can examine their vocabulary curricula and choose relevant and key concepts for such a lesson from the reading selections. For example, biology teachers can engage the class in exploring and investigating the vocabulary of muscles (Blasingame Jr. & Nilsen, 2005) as students learn the literal and metaphorical meanings of the words related to muscles as well as related biological and physiological terms.

Sonia, a tenth-grade mathematics teacher, teaches a class of ELL students with varied English language proficiency levels. Because she has relied on alphabetized glossaries or isolated word selection from word problems or the textbook, her efforts have been largely unsuccessful.

One day Sonia read an article on heart rate which directly applied to the topic of her day's lesson. She was intrigued by not only the fascinating facts presented by the article but also by the possibilities of using the basic word *heart* to take students on a journey to learn both literal and metaphorical usages associated with it.

Sonia started her lesson by talking with her students about the word *heart* (Figure 17).

**Figure 17: Reading about a Heart**

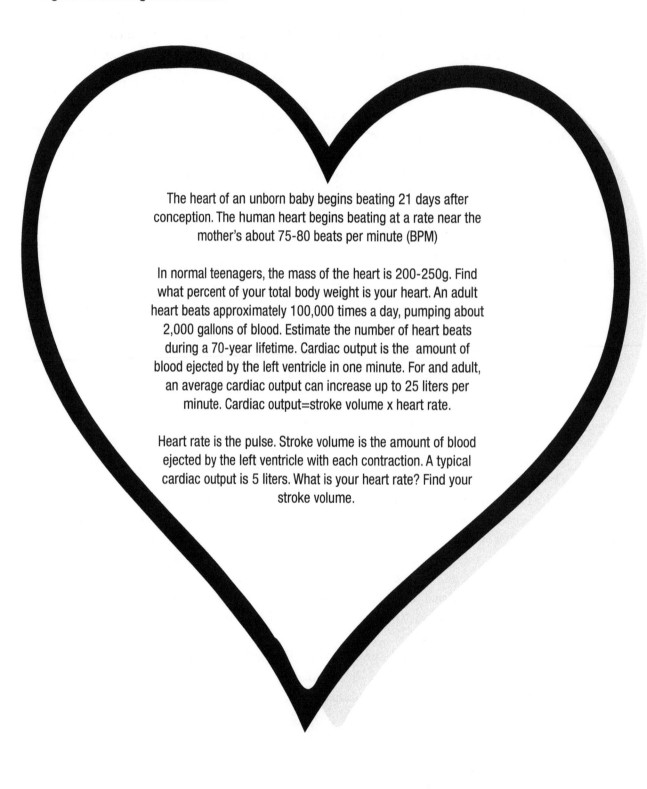

The heart of an unborn baby begins beating 21 days after conception. The human heart begins beating at a rate near the mother's about 75-80 beats per minute (BPM)

In normal teenagers, the mass of the heart is 200-250g. Find what percent of your total body weight is your heart. An adult heart beats approximately 100,000 times a day, pumping about 2,000 gallons of blood. Estimate the number of heart beats during a 70-year lifetime. Cardiac output is the amount of blood ejected by the left ventricle in one minute. For and adult, an average cardiac output can increase up to 25 liters per minute. Cardiac output=stroke volume x heart rate.

Heart rate is the pulse. Stroke volume is the amount of blood ejected by the left ventricle with each contraction. A typical cardiac output is 5 liters. What is your heart rate? Find your stroke volume.

Teacher: You think the heart is the most important. And every culture has that belief. There's no culture who thinks, "Oh, heart, big deal. What about liver?"

Class: [affirming responses]

Teacher: "I have love for you in my liver." We don't say that. I put some expressions that are in English that are very, very common. You can hear them all the time unless you don't hear them because you don't understand. So I put these expressions; they all have the word *heart* in them. And I just want to see how many of them you know, and if you don't know we gonna put the definitions together. Cause, again, they're so common. So...*to have a heart*, what does it mean? It means that you have an organ for pumping blood?

Student A: That I have a very...important organ.

Teacher: Yeah, I don't think it means that. To have a heart.

Student B: Poor.

Teacher: To be poor!

Student C: [emphatically with raised voice] No! Human!

Teacher: To be human? Uh, animals don't have hearts?

Student D: Mammals.

Class: [inaudible murmurings]

Teacher: To be a mammal? So *have a heart*—what does it mean? To be kind and to be nice. Have a heart. To have a heart is to be nice. *To know something by heart?* Raise your hand. Luis? What do you think it is to *know something by heart?*"

Luis: To live it.

Student E: To leave it?

Student F: To see something.

Teacher: To see something? Uh, I tell you something. I know a few things by heart. I know my name by heart. I know the English alphabet by heart. I know multiplication tables by heart. What does it mean to know something by heart?

Student G: Expert.

Teacher: To be an expert? It's about memory. It's about remembering. So *to know something by heart*—what does it mean?"

Student H: Memorize.

Teacher: Memorize without looking, right? So what do you remember by heart?

Student I: Nothing.

Teacher: You remember nothing by heart? Oh, poor thing.

Class: [calling out answers, inaudible]

Teacher: So you should remember this by heart [gesturing to top of handout].

The heart lesson was a hit. Sonia's students were so fascinated by the extended expressions and metaphorical meanings associated with the word *heart* that they did a class investigation to collect more associated expressions and present them on word posters like this (Figure 18).

**Figure 18: Heart-related Expressions**

| Expression | Picture | Meaning |
|---|---|---|
| A broken heart |  | Sad feelings |
| Heart of gold |  | Kind and generous |
| Heavy heart |  | Sad and sorrowful |
| Heart and soul |  | Strong feeling and dedication |
| Heart goes out |  | Feel sorry and sympathetic |
| Heart to heart |  | Speaking openly and intimately about something private |

To Sonia, mathematics learning is just as much language and culture based as any other subjects. Even though many mathematical concepts are universal, the way to do mathematics and mathematics expressions vary from language to language and culture to culture. So she views herself as a language teacher and often conducts a vocabulary mini-lesson first before tackling mathematical problems. The previous discussion captured Sonia's vocabulary teaching moment when she creatively used the reading material to increase her students' understanding of the meaning of *heart*. After the students gained a deeper understanding about the word, Sonia began teaching the mathematical topic of plotting by modeling and asking students to plot those numbers presented in the reading.

## Using Inquiry-oriented Discussion to Explore Concepts

In an inquiry-oriented class discussion, the teacher asks exploratory questions to open up the discussion about the meaning of a new concept or word without explicitly giving out the definition. In these discussions, students take a journey of meaning making with the teacher. In the beginning, students do not know which concept or word is under study, so they are more responsive to the teacher's open-ended questions. They follow the instructor's train of thought to question, argue, hypothesize, and synthesize ideas to arrive at the concept and meaning of the actual word.

This well-established teaching practice used in many subject-matter classes across academic disciplines generally yields good results in developing students' critical-thinking skills and conceptual knowledge. Yet, although research has shown the benefit of inquiry-oriented, teacher-led discussions to engage students critically and deeply in comprehending subject-matter knowledge, inquiry-oriented discussion is not frequently used to teach vocabulary. Instead, because of time and curriculum pressures, many subject-matter teachers find themselves tempted to just give out the word list with definitions or assign students the task of finding the word meaning in the dictionary on their own rather than investigating the word in depth in class.

Even if a teacher begins an inquiry-oriented discussion in class, it often occurs during a rapid-fire question-and-answer sequence, which leaves some students—especially ELLs—with very little time to think about the questions. In addition, the discussion is often de-contextualized and beyond their comprehension capabilities. When new words emerge in the discussion or in the teacher's questions, ELLs quickly get lost after the discussion begins and have trouble participating.

Finally, ELL students who come from cultures in which teacher talk is the only talk valued in class often fail to understand the importance of inquiry-oriented learning and the value of their responses and those of their peers.

Therefore, the first steps in inquiry-oriented discussion is for the teacher to communicate the importance of such a discussion to their ELLs, plan such a discussion carefully to make sure that the questions are engaging and comprehensible to their ELLs, and prepare them to participate in such a discussion.

**Tips for successful inquiry-oriented discussions.** Inquiry-based vocabulary teaching requires the teacher to focus on one or two key concepts and guide students in discussing the meaning of unknown words themselves through talking, questioning, debating, and thinking. An effective inquiry-based vocabulary discussion includes the following features:

- The word concept of the selected word or words is complex enough to be worthy of discussion.
- Teacher questions are phrased carefully to ensure comprehension. They are open-ended in order to invite students' original responses. To make sure ELLs can participate, it's good practice to prepare several follow-up questions for clarification and to reframe the key questions.
- The teacher refrains from giving out the word definition early. The discussion and learning process are the goals of this approach. Positive comments along the way will encourage students to explore the concept.
- Questions are written and given to ELLs before the discussion for additional support. Teachers also can give out possible sentence starters and let students write down their responses.
- The value of this American educational practice is explicitly taught so that these students won't be confused about or fail to see the point of having such discussions.
- Enough wait time is given for student responses. Teachers watch out for possible new words that emerge during the discussion and provide language support for ELLs when they have difficulty following along.

Look at the following example of such a discussion in a ninth-grade biology class in which the teacher teaches the concept of *adaptation*. The class is composed of all ELLs at different levels of English language proficiency. Mark, the biology teacher, uses a series of pictures of various animals, such as a giraffe, hawk, duck, polar bear, ermine, etc. to facilitate the discussion as follows (Dong, 2004).

| Teacher: | Take a look at this picture. What is this? |
|----------|---------------------------------------------|
| Sam: | A polar bear. |
| Teacher: | Do you know any bears besides polar bears? |
| Philip: | Black bears. |
| Teacher: | Where do black bears live? |
| Philip: | In the jungle. |
| Teacher: | Where do polar bears live? |
| Rachel: | In a very cold place. |
| Megan: | In the Arctic. |
| Teacher: | Right, in the Arctic. Why are the different kinds of bears found in different parts of the world? Why aren't all bears found in the same place of the world? |
| Li Ann: | Because the weather is not the same. |
| Teacher: | Why is that? |
| Li Ann: | Polar bears can only live in the cold place. |
| Teacher: | How so? |

| Yong: | Because look at the picture here, the ice and the snow. |
|---|---|
| Kadisha: | Black bears cannot survive in that cold. |
| Teacher: | What does a polar bear do to survive the cold? |
| Kamal: | They have fur, white fur. Black bears do not have that thick fur and their fur is black. |
| Teacher: | Interesting. How come a polar bear's fur is white? |
| Sam: | They have to hide to blend in? |
| Teacher: | You are saying that they use the white fur to defend themselves? |
| Dan: | The white color is also transparent to sunlight and keeps them warm. |
| Teacher: | OK, so the polar bear's fur and the color of the fur are for some special adaptation purposes. Let's look at this picture. What is going on here? |
| Patricia: | The duck is swimming in the river. |
| Teacher: | What kind of environment does a duck live in? |
| Carlos: | It's warm and close to the water. |
| Fidel: | Ducks have fur, too. |
| Teacher: | Is that fur? |
| Kamal: | I don't think so. How can it have fur if it lives in a warm climate? |
| Dan: | I know what it's called. |
| Zoila: | It's feather not fur. |
| Teacher: | Why does it have feathers? |
| Zoila: | Feather helps it move, swim. |
| Teacher: | What is the fur's function? |
| Dmitri: | Fur keeps bears warm. |
| Teacher: | So why do ducks have feathers and polar bears have fur? |
| Sam: | Because they have different functions. |
| Dmitri: | I know—because they have to adapt to their environments. (99-100) |

In the beginning, Mark's questions were simple and open-ended to activate students' prior knowledge:

What is this (referring to the picture of a polar bear)?

Do you know any bears besides polar bears (after learning that some of his ELLs do not know what a polar bear is)?

Where do black bears live? Where do polar bears live?

Why are different kinds of bears found in different parts of the world?

Why aren't all bears found in the same place of the world?

When Mark noticed that students arrived at the critical part of the discussion, he paraphrased these responses to highlight key concepts like "You are saying that they use the white fur to defend themselves?" Or "So the polar bear's fur and the color of the fur are for some special adaptation purposes." Paraphrasing in this way keeps the class focused on the topic and helps students crystallize the concept as the discussion progresses.

Once students connected the word *fur* with the polar bear's survival function, Mark directed the class' attention to the duck. This example was used to help students think about an animal's response to its environment. At this point, some students were confused about the feather and fur concepts. Even when the students' responses were incorrect, as when they were discussing the words *feather* and *fur*, Mark didn't ask students to look into dictionaries, but rather, asked questions (*Is that fur?*; *Why does it have feathers?*; and *What is the fur's function?*) to issue an invitation for further discussion on the meaning and function of these words. His questions allow the students to figure out the differences between the two words on their own. In doing so, Mark not only expands students' scientific knowledge but also stretches their language abilities.

Once the meaning of *adaptation* is understood, students work as a group to make a table of the animals in the pictures and their adaptive features in the environment. This table shows what the group can produce (Table 4: Dong, 2004: pp. 100).

**Table 4: Animal Adaptation Comparisons**

| Animal | Adaptation | Function | Ecosystem |
|--------|-----------|----------|-----------|
| Giraffe | A long neck | To catch food | Grassland and forest |
| Hawk | A sharp beak, large eyes | To hunt for food | Forest |
| Duck | Large feet and a wide mouth | To swim and to catch fish | Water |
| Armadillo | Hard shell | To protect itself from other animals | Desert |
| Ermine | Changing color of the fur and a long tail | To defend itself | Grassland |
| Polar bear | White fur | To keep warm | Arctic |

# Word Graphic Organizers

A word graphic organizer visually organizes and represents one or more words. Often called *word maps*, *webs*, *diagrams*, or *charts*, these organizers are commonly used in the classroom across academic disciplines. They stimulate students to think about the relationships between the word under study and other words. They organize and present different aspects of the word in a compact and visual manner that highlights key information about the word. They are also easy to learn and use, and students respond well to them.

ELLs face an overwhelming amount of vocabulary demanded by different subjects. Also, as beginning second-language learners, they have a tendency to get lost in the sea of unfamiliar words, losing sight of the relationships among the words and the big concepts that the words present. For ELLs, graphic organizers hold special appeal because they focus and organize the learning and make it visual and manageable. They also highlight key concepts so that students can effectively learn groups of words that are organized around a central concept.

Word graphic organizers can be centered around an individual word visually represented one at a time or with a group of words to illustrate inter-relationships. Organizers can be used at different points of instruction: at the beginning to introduce the new word or concept and to activate prior knowledge; in the middle of instruction to facilitate comprehension, resolve confusion, organize a large amount of material, and crystallize understanding; and near the end to consolidate thinking and review.

Care should be taken to plan and develop meaningful and effective word graphic organizers. Teachers should always adapt existing graphic organizers to meet their students' needs and to add creativity and imagination to the thinking process. Mindless graphic organizer fill-ins should be avoided. The thought processes—like the rationale and context for the chosen words to generate a graphic organizer—should be articulated by students throughout to highlight the relationships among the words. Following is an example of a social studies teacher's creative use of word graphic organizers.

**Single-word graphic organizer: word web/map.** A word web or map is a strategy that develops both associative thinking skills and a general concept of the word under study. It can be used as a pre-reading or beginning lesson activity or as a prewriting activity to activate students' prior knowledge and brainstorm ideas for writing.

The teacher begins by drawing a circle around the new word and asking the class for associations with questions like *What comes to mind when you think of this word? What are some of the words related to this word? What does this word mean?*

The teacher includes as many associations as possible from the class. Then, she brings the class' attention to the word in the context of the lesson to uncover the word's deeper meanings. The teacher can also engage the class in grouping the words in categories and asking why certain words belong together.

For a prewriting activity, the teacher can ask students to develop word clusters based on the associations and organize those clusters according to their functional use and context. This way, students will be armed with the key concept or idea to focus their writing and also receive solid language support to get them started. Following is a sample word web on the concept of texture discussed in an art classroom (Figure 19).

**Figure 19: Word Web of *Texture***

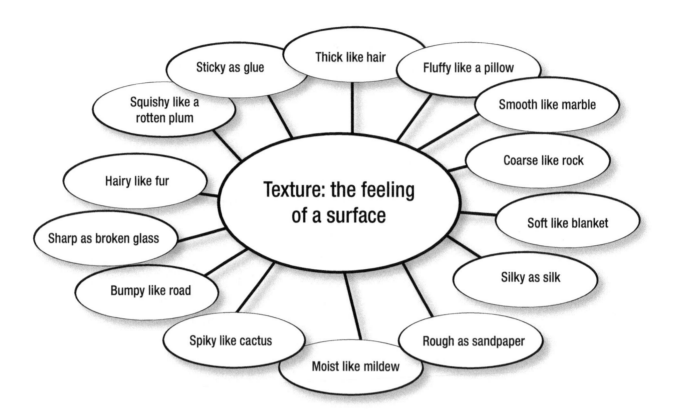

**Single-word graphic organizer: word square.** A word square is a graphic organizer composed of four squares, with each square describing one aspect of the word. It can be used at various points of instruction to develop students' in-depth understanding of vocabulary under study. When used appropriately, it can also promote students' interest in word learning as well as creative- and critical-thinking skills.

Dictionaries and thesauruses should be available when doing this activity. ELLs should be encouraged to include their native-language translations of the word to reinforce understanding. Teacher modeling is necessary before the activity.

**Steps**
1. Students divide into groups of three or five.
2. Each group chooses a word for which to compose a word square.
3. Students in the group design a vocabulary square, created by dividing a large square into four equal blocks. Students complete the four squares by:
    - Defining the word and supplying pronunciation, etymology, and parts of speech.
    - Illustrating the word's meaning
    - Writing a synonym and antonym of the word and using the word and its equivalents in other languages.
    - Writing a sentence using the word.

4. Each group shares its word with the class. Groups are also encouraged to talk about the thinking process: Why did they draw the picture they drew? How did they come up with the etymology, parts of speech, and connotation of the word? What did they learn about this word that they didn't know before? Sharing is important here to encourage students to articulate their thought processes and justify their responses in order to achieve a deeper understanding.

Word squares can be posted on the wall to showcase students' work and to use as reinforcement for meaningful and contextualized language learning. Teachers can also launch a creative project on language use in the real world by assigning students to collect as many word usages related to what they just studied as possible and to investigate the various contexts and social situations in which these words are used in real life (Figures 20 and 21).

**Figure 20: Word Square of _Dominant_**

| **Meaning, Etymology, Parts of Speech, and Pronunciation** | **Synonyms and Antonyms** |
|---|---|
| Meaning: Controlling, having great power and influence | Synonyms: controlling, ruling, commanding |
| | Antonyms: humble, modest, reserved |
| Latin: _dominus_ | **In Other Languages** |
| | Spanish: dominante |
| Part of Speech: adjective | French: dominant |
| | Chinese: 控制 |
| Pronunciation: /ˈdɑmənənt/ | Greek: δεσπόζουσα |

### Dominant

| **Image** | **Our Sentence** |
|---|---|
|  | The king was dominant over his kingdom. |
| | Julius Caesar was a dominant king. |

**Figure 21: Word Square of *Apparition***

| Meaning, Etymology, Parts of Speech, and Pronunciation | Synonyms and Antonyms |
|---|---|
| Meaning: a spirit of the dead appearing<br><br>Latin: *apparit*<br><br>Part of Speech: noun<br><br>Pronunciation: /æpə`rɪʃən/ | Synonyms: ghost, spirit, supernatural being<br><br>Antonyms: being, reality, fact<br><br>**In Other Languages**<br>Polish: Objawienie<br>Spanish: aparición<br>Chinese: 幻影<br>Korean: 유령 |

| **Apparition** ||
|---|---|
| **Image**<br> | **Our Sentence**<br>We were told that house was haunted by the apparition. |

Of course, the teacher can adjust the content of the four squares to the lesson's learning objectives and students' needs. For example, a science teacher may want to focus on the distinction between the key concept and other concepts by having students generate examples and non-examples of the term under study as shown below (Figure 22).

**Figure 22: Word Square of *Lever***

| Word | Examples |
|---|---|
| Lever<br><br>**Definition**<br>A thing that is used with a fixed point to increase the force to move something else. | screwdriver<br>hammer<br>nutcracker<br>faucet<br>diving board |
| **Non-examples**<br>door<br>key<br>hair clip<br>stairs<br>clock | **Picture**  |

**Single-word graphic organizer: concept wheel.** A concept wheel is a circle divided into different sections, with the keyword/concept placed in the center. Students are asked to find word associations with the concept and complete the sections based on their reading. Lisa, a ninth-grade English teacher, is teaching James McBride's *The Color of Water*. Aware of the lack of possible cultural background knowledge of all her students in general, and especially her newly mainstreamed ELLs, Lisa decided to focus on major conceptual words as a way to build the necessary background knowledge for students to critically read and understand the novel.

Students work together in groups to select keywords in the reading, gather relevant information about the word under study, and present the results to the class (Figure 23). The concept wheel includes the following elements:

- Citation from the reading
- Word picture
- Word meaning (contextual meaning and dictionary meaning)
- Word history
- Word evolution
- Other words related to this word
- Word connotation

**Figure 23: Concept Wheel of a Hippie**

Word Study in James McBrides' *The Color of Water*

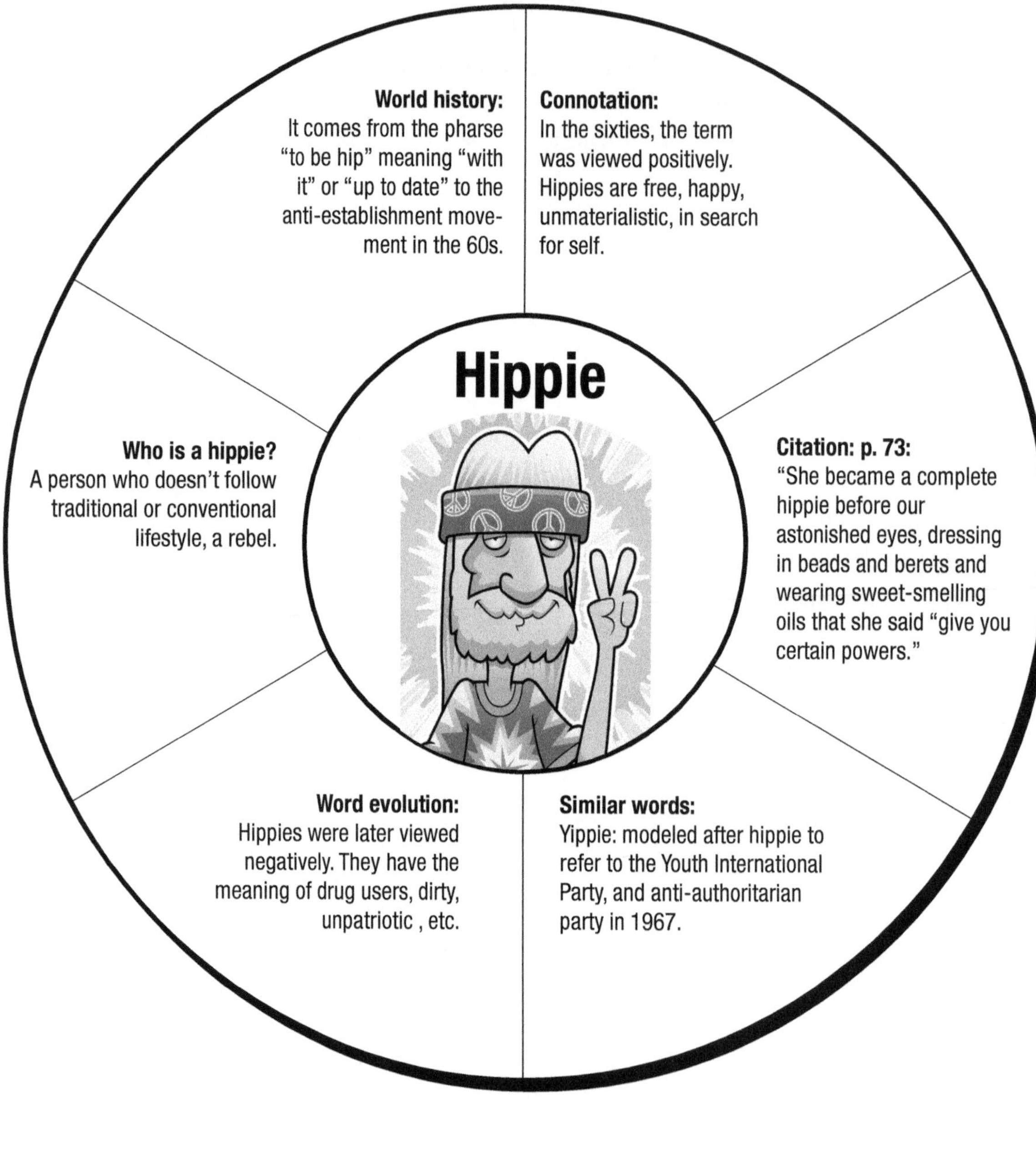

**World history:**
It comes from the pharse "to be hip" meaning "with it" or "up to date" to the anti-establishment movement in the 60s.

**Connotation:**
In the sixties, the term was viewed positively. Hippies are free, happy, unmaterialistic, in search for self.

**Who is a hippie?**
A person who doesn't follow traditional or conventional lifestyle, a rebel.

# Hippie

**Citation: p. 73:**
"She became a complete hippie before our astonished eyes, dressing in beads and berets and wearing sweet-smelling oils that she said "give you certain powers.""

**Word evolution:**
Hippies were later viewed negatively. They have the meaning of drug users, dirty, unpatriotic , etc.

**Similar words:**
Yippie: modeled after hippie to refer to the Youth International Party, and anti-authoritarian party in 1967.

# Multiple-word Graphic Organizers

These graphic organizers involve more than one unfamiliar word or concept. Because they help students to clarify thinking, are especially helpful when teaching complex and inter-related concepts. A well-thought-out multiple-word graphic organizer provides a visual and intellectual way for students to study the varied concepts and relationships among the words.

It is especially important to use this type of graphic organizer to move vocabulary learning from a focused study of individual words or concepts to a study of how these words or concepts are categorized, organized, and related to one another. This graphic organizer is often used during the lesson or as a review for exams. Students use it to visualize the relationship between concepts, perceive the words in a different manner, and verbalize their thought processes as they go along.

Teachers should model the strategy and verbalize their thought processes while completing a sample graphic organizer. Group work with this organizer is especially valuable because students will gain valuable experience interacting with peers to air and develop their ideas verbally as they move through their thought processes.

Linda, a ninth-grade biology teacher, does not want to use a graphic organizer as busy work for students. She believes that a graphic organizer should be used only when students are challenged by the complexity and difficulty of scientific language. She also believes that students should be involved in developing graphic organizers in addition to filling them in.

Some of the scientific vocabulary, according to Linda, cannot be internalized without seeing and manipulating it through pictures and words. Making that scientific knowledge visible with a graphic organizer is a bonus for ELLs because they are simultaneously learning both language and content. Following is an example of a graphic organizer generated by Linda's students (Figure 24).

**Figure 24: Food Chain Visualization**

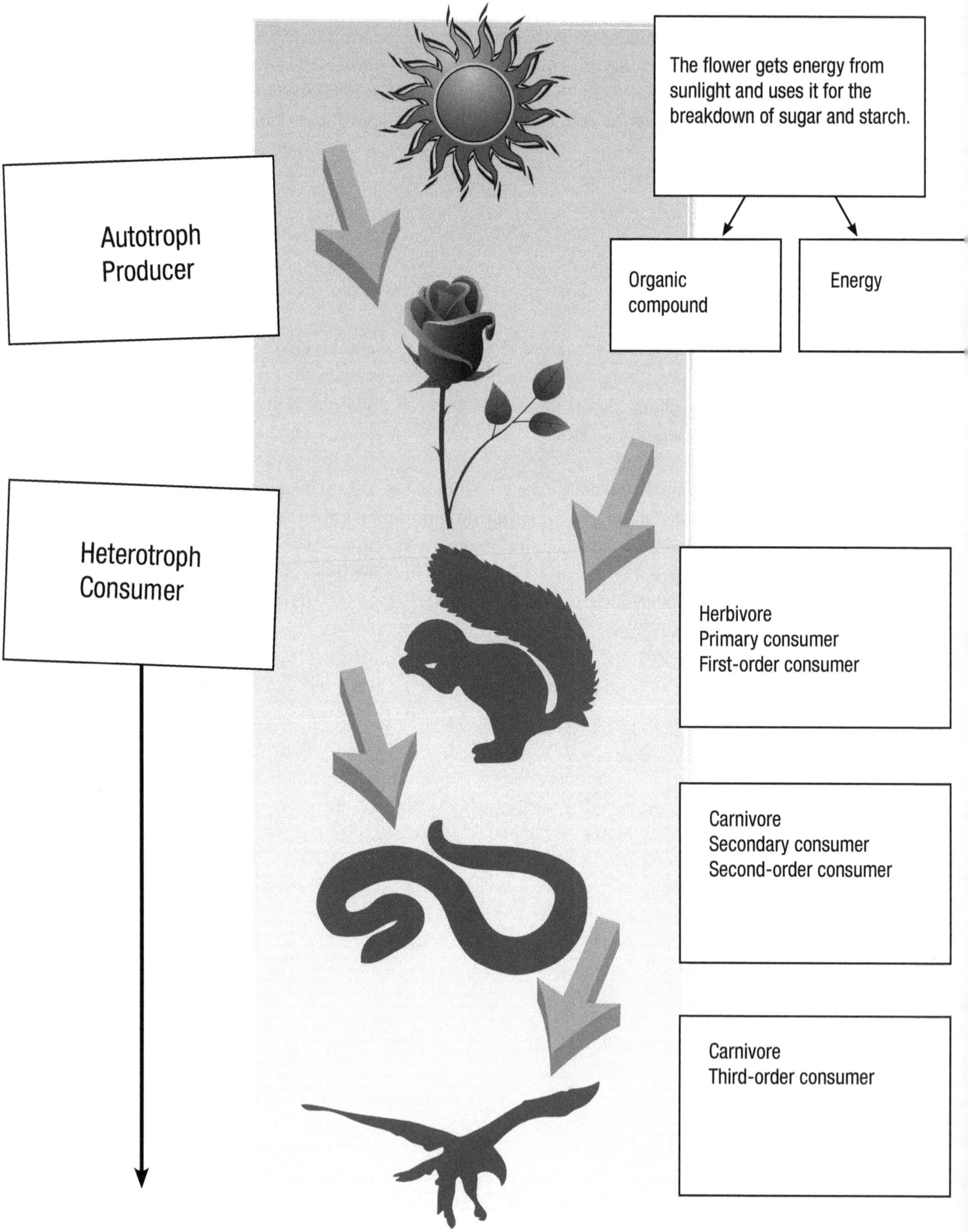

Autotroph
Producer

Heterotroph
Consumer

The flower gets energy from sunlight and uses it for the breakdown of sugar and starch.

Organic compound

Energy

Herbivore
Primary consumer
First-order consumer

Carnivore
Secondary consumer
Second-order consumer

Carnivore
Third-order consumer

**Multiple-word graphic organizer: category chart.** Before tutoring an eleventh-grade ELL, Dan read over the text that discussed the three types of American colonies. He found the language difficult and beyond his tutee's language proficiency level. To help her understand and prepare for the upcoming test on the subject, Dan used a graphic organizer: a chart to describe the three types of colonies and their functions. He added examples to compare and contrast those keywords, like *charter*, *proprietary*, *royal*, *political*, *economic*, and *social* (Table 5). In doing so, Dan made the subject matter manageable for his tutee and focused on the concepts.

**Table 5: Three Types of Colonies**

| Area of control | Charter | Proprietary | Royal |
|---|---|---|---|
| **Political:** How to govern and make policies | Church members chose legislators (lawmakers) and governors | Colonists chose legislators, owners, and governor of colony; requirement for voting | Large land owners own plantations; high property recruitment; king of England chose governor |
| **Economic:** How to produce, sell, and purchase goods and food | Rocky New England soil—not good for farming, timber, fur and merchant traders | Colonies produced a lot of wheat; also there was mining in Penn. | Tobacco as key; servants and slaves worked in the field |
| **Social:** How to relate to others in the community and get along | No freedom of religion, but strict Puritan laws (strictness and austerity in conduct, opposed to sensual pleasures) | Lots of different religions, such as Quakers (those who believed in equality, not authority) in Penn. | Catholics permitted large differences between plantation owners and small farmers |

**Multiple-word graphic organizer: iceberg-metaphor organizer.** Teachers can use the iceberg metaphor to explore and teach complex literary vocabulary like external and emotional character traits. In doing so, students focus not only on the character's appearance and behaviors, but also on what may be implied in the text about their less visible character traits. This process moves students to a deeper understanding of the text as they make inferences and use a variety of vocabulary to describe the characters. Students are guided to explore the character from multiple dimensions and to pay attention to subtle subtexts that are not easily apparent. Critical reading results, as shown in the following table and figure (Table 6 and Figure 25).

## Table 6: Invisible and Visible Character Traits

| Character | Visible characteristics | Textual support | Invisible characteristics | Textual support |
|---|---|---|---|---|
| Sally | Beautiful | "paint your eyes like Cleopatra" | Rebellious at school | "You pull your skirt straight." |
| | Lonely | "No one to lend you her hairbrush." | Obedient | "rub the blue paint off your eye-lids" |
| | | "you don't have a best friend to lean against the schoolyard fence with" | Desperate for love | "You look at your feet and walk fast to the house you can't come out from." |
| | Dreamer | "you like to dream and dream" | | "all you wanted, Sally, was to love" |
| | Sad | Without any friends: "You lean against the schoolyard fence alone…" | | |
| | Fierce | Just had a fight with the best friend. | | |
| Sally's father | Very strict and traditional | "To be this beautiful is trouble." | Not affectionate | "You could close your eyes and you wouldn't have to worry what people said because you never belonged." |
| | Religious | "They are very strict in his religion. They are not supposed to dance…She can't go out." | Having no communication with his daughter | "nobody could make you sad and nobody would think you're strange" |

**Figure 25: Character Trait Iceberg**

(Character Study from *The House on Mango Street*)

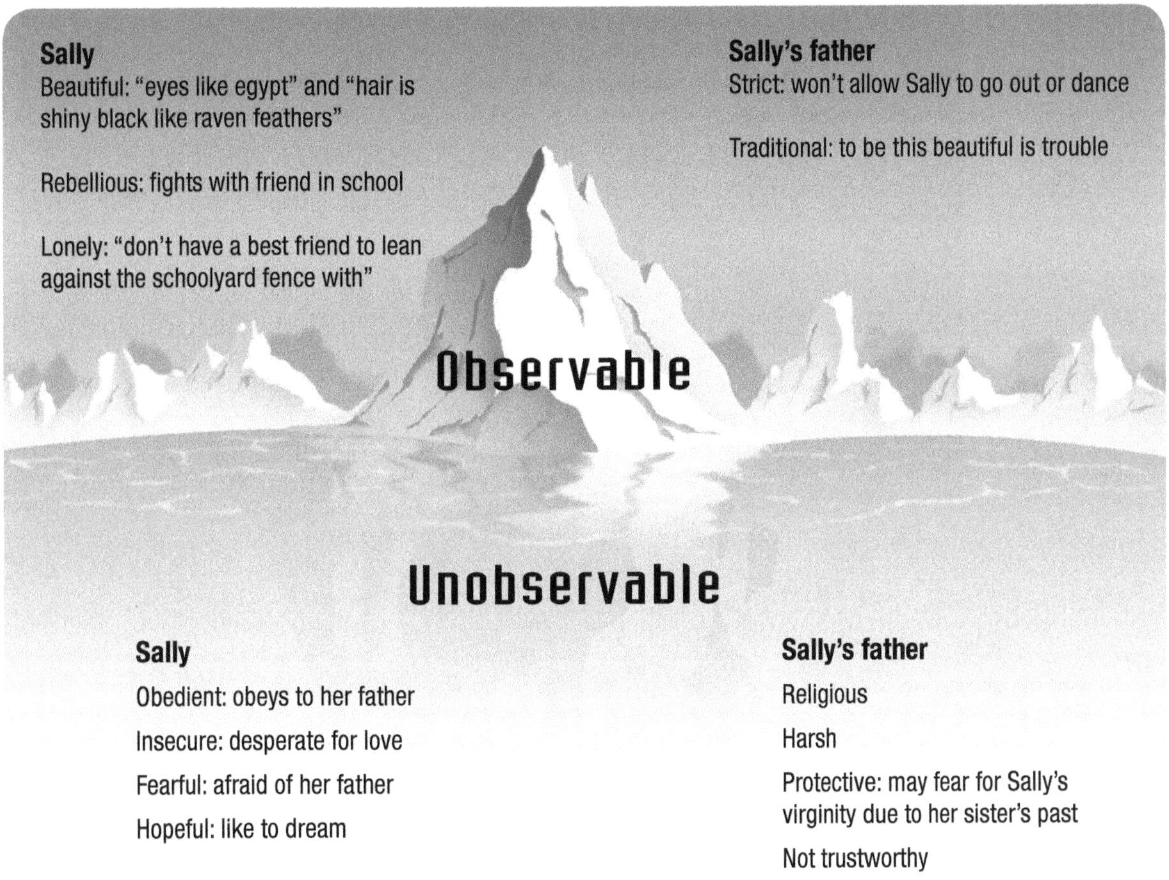

**Sally**
Beautiful: "eyes like egypt" and "hair is shiny black like raven feathers"

Rebellious: fights with friend in school

Lonely: "don't have a best friend to lean against the schoolyard fence with"

**Sally's father**
Strict: won't allow Sally to go out or dance

Traditional: to be this beautiful is trouble

**Observable**

**Unobservable**

**Sally**
Obedient: obeys to her father

Insecure: desperate for love

Fearful: afraid of her father

Hopeful: like to dream

**Sally's father**
Religious

Harsh

Protective: may fear for Sally's virginity due to her sister's past

Not trustworthy

# CHAPTER 4
## Interacting with New Words in a Rich Context

• • • • •

*The difference between the right word and almost the right word is the difference between lightning and a lightning bug.*
—*Mark Twain*

As we have already seen, interacting with new words in a rich context is one of the most effective instructional strategies for vocabulary acquisition. Rather than passively copying down the definition and memorizing it for the test, students need to interact with the new word through multiple senses to experience it—including using physical movements.

The new word should be learned in context rather than in isolation. The context can be a reading passage where the word is situated, a creative environment where the word is involved (such as using the senses of feeling, seeing, hearing, touching, and smelling), or an in-depth study of the social and cultural meaning of the word. In this chapter, I discuss and illustrate how teachers can engage students in interacting with the new word and learning it in a context-rich environment.

## The Keyword Method

We know that ELLs entering American schools at the secondary level must play an urgent game of catch-up to acquire academic vocabulary. At the secondary level, many of the academic and disciplinary-specific words are abstract and complicated and often cannot be learned by a picture or definition alone. The keyword method focuses on making associations and highlighting meaning.

This strategy provides an effective mnemonic tool that helps learners actively seek word meaning, apply what they already know to learn the new word, think about the new word in a unique and creative way, and remember the word. This strategy can help ELLs actively learn words and learn how to make associations independently.

The teacher models the process first by examining the vocabulary under study for possible keyword candidates and discussing her choices with the students. A good keyword appears within a new word and is linked to the new word in some ways. The keyword can either look or sound like the new word.

Once the keyword is selected, the teacher can first model and then ask students to create an image to enhance understanding and retention. Students can then write about the association between the keyword and the new word. Once the teacher models how it is done, students can be coached to create varied keywords. For example, as chosen by students, the keywords for *perspective* can be *spec* or *inspec*t.

After the keywords are chosen, students need to make an association between the word and the new word by describing how they are linked. Then they create a visual image of the keyword to demonstrate its connection with the actual word for comprehension and recall. Finally, students should always be asked to give the rationale for their keyword. (See the Appendices for word examples that subject-matter teachers can use.)

The keyword strategy takes time for teachers to model and for students to learn. Research, however, has shown its long-term effectiveness, especially in developing independent word-learning skills. Teachers should set aside time in class regularly to practice one keyword at a time and encourage students to think creatively about the new word.

Here are examples of words learned using the keyword method (Figures 26, 27, and 28):

**Figures 26, 27, and 28: Keyword on *Amendment*, *Segregate*, and *Perspective***

| **Your word:** Amendment |
| --- |
| **Keyword:** Mend: change or repair |
| **Rationale for the keyword:** *Amend* means *change or modify something*. So *amendment* is the action of making changes or writing a document that makes changes to the original document; e.g., U.S. Bill of Rights, the first ten amendments to the U.S. Constitution. |
| **Image or picture of your keyword:**  |
| **Create a sentence with your word:** The student government added an amendment to the school policy to reduce homework on the weekends. |

| |
|---|
| **Your word:** |
| Segregate |
| **Keyword:** |
| Gate |
| **Rationale for the keyword:** |
| The gate is what we use to keep something or somebody out. So *segregate* is to separate because of race, gender, or religion. |
| **Image or picture of your keyword:** |
|   |
| **Create a sentence with your word:** |
| In our school, special education students are no longer segregated from regular students. |

| |
|---|
| **Your word:** |
| Perspective |
| **Keyword:** |
| spec—glasses |
| **Rationale for the keyword:** |
| Specs tell us about something we see. So *perspective* is all about what we see. |
| **Image or picture of your keyword:** |
|  |
| **Your sentence:** |
| I put on my specs to get a better perspective on the world. |

Pan, a biology education pre-service teacher, teaches a group of tenth-grade ELLs. In her unit on muscles, Pan uses the keyword activity, assigning her students to go to local gyms to find creative ways to memorize those words about muscles (Figure 29).

**Figure 29: Keyword on *Abdominal***

| |
|---|
| **Your word:** <br> Abdominal: the muscles of the abdomen |
| **Keyword:** <br> Domino |
| **Rationale for the keyword:** <br> The abdominal muscle is where the Domino's pizza goes. |
| **Image or picture of your keyword:** <br>  |
| **Your sentence:** <br> After dancing so hard for the night, Sally pulled her abdominal muscle. |

# Word Total Physical Response (TPR)

The effective second-language teaching strategy known as Total Physical Response (TPR) was developed in the late 1970s. It is based on the principle that children learn their first language through movement and listening before any speaking can take place. Many second-language learners stress out about speaking English and fear the demands of verbal expressions in class. TPR is a method to reduce anxiety and promote learning in a natural and context-rich way. TPR also parallels Gardner's multiple intelligences theory in that it engages students' non-verbal intelligences and strengths to learn when they are not yet ready to use their verbal intelligence.

In the original TPR-oriented learning, the teacher gives the students a series of verbal commands, and students listen and act out these commands using physical movements. TPR is especially effective when teaching basic vocabulary—such as concrete, action, and emotional words—to ELLs who are at the beginning level. It can also be adapted to teach even abstract or complex words. The teacher orchestrates students to experience the concept using body language and involves their imaginations and creativity to dramatize and show the concept without verbalizing it.

**TPR to teach *diffusion*.** To experience the concept of diffusion, for example, a group of science pre-service teachers arranged students to sit on two sides of the classroom. One side had many students and the other had fewer. Teachers then asked their students to role-play molecules by standing up and walking around in all different directions in the classroom. Through the movement, students bumped into each other in a confined space (the classroom) to experience how molecules collide and move in a zigzag fashion in the diffusion process. Finally, the teachers asked the class to stop moving and look at their surroundings to understand the concept of diffusion: how molecules move from high concentration (students crowded on one side of the classroom) to low concentration (students now are all scattered around the classroom).

**TPR to teach *interdependence*.** To illustrate the concept of interdependence, a group of social studies pre-service teachers asked the whole class to stand up and form a circle. Students were told to hold each other's hands. Next, the teachers asked students to stop holding hands and stand on one leg to see how long they could balance standing still. In no time at all, students were wobbling and lost their balance.

Students were then asked to return to their original positions and once again hold hands. The teachers asked the class to reflect on why they could not stand still on one leg on their own without holding hands with their neighbors and what it means to have neighbors' hands to hold on to.

**TPR to teach *ecosystems*.** Mike, a pre-service science teacher, used TPR to teach a lesson on the concept of ecosystems to a class of ELL ninth graders. Before the lesson, he prepared a deck of index cards. On each card, he wrote down an animal or plant's name and its survival needs, such as the kind of food they eat. In class, he asked every student to choose an index card and stand in a circle with everyone holding their cards up so all could see.

He randomly picked a student and gave her a long strand of yarn, asking her to pass the yarn to another student whose card represented the food that his or her animal needed to eat. For example, if the chosen student representing a cow and its survival needs was eating grass, then she would pass the other end of the yarn to the student representing grass. That student would then pass the yarn to another student who represented sun and water.

As the yarn is passed, students see a food web forming among them. After a few rounds of yarn passing, Mike used scissors to cut one part of the yarn and asked the class to think about what would happen to their ecosystem now that it is broken. Finally, students were encouraged to write about this from the perspective of their animal or plant.

Below are some student examples from the following writing assignment prompt: "When the food chain (string) is cut or broken, how is your animal or organism affected in the ecosystem? What can cause this? If it is not fixed, what would be the end result?"

> If my plants don't have sunlight, they will die. Then the cows have nothing to eat, and they will die. As a human, I will have no beef to eat, and I have to stay on a vegetable diet only.

> I'm a cow. I need to eat grass in order to live. Without it, I won't produce milk, and I'll die. Because of it, people don't get to drink milk or eat cheese anymore. If I die, people will not have meat to eat, and they may starve.

> I'm a caterpillar. I eat leaves and grass to survive. If there is no grass left or plants, then I'll have nothing to eat. If I die of hunger, birds who feed on me will die as well.

## Word Collocation

Word collocation, or grouping, works well for ELLs. Research shows that people acquire language not by learning one isolated word at a time but by acquiring words that often go together or are found in language clusters. Word clusters or combinations facilitate retention because our brains are more likely to remember language in chunks or blocks rather than as single, isolated words. For example, the word *conflict* is often used in combinations of phrases, such as *have a conflict, create a conflict, solve a conflict*, etc.

Native English speakers draw on their solid oral-language background, cultural knowledge, or past reading and class discussions to figure out these word combinations on their own. ELLs, though, are often too overwhelmed by the task of trying to figure out an individual word in the reading to pay attention to related words that surround that word. Teachers, therefore, need to teach and train ELLs to identify and use word collocation to learn vocabulary.

Teachers also need to be aware that many English word combinations are culturally and language specific. Because the combinations often are different from those in the ELL's native languages, an initial encounter of the English word combinations can be confusing. Students need additional time to pay conscious attention to recognize and learn the new word combinations in English.

The following are examples of a few collocation comparisons between English and other languages:

| | |
|---|---|
| English | have a party |
| Arabic | make a party |
| | |
| English | have a good diet |
| Chinese | make a good diet |
| | |
| English | pay attention to |
| French | make attention at |
| | |
| English | resolve a conflict |
| German | finish a conflict |
| | |
| English | run a store |
| Polish | drive a store |

**Clustering words.** Word collocation can also be used to teach related word clusters. In this way, students build a habit of looking at the context of the new word to see how it is used with other words in reading, writing, and speaking, which makes the process of learning new vocabulary easier.

In addition, when assigning students verbal or writing exercises, some commonly found, discipline-specific word clusters or phrases should be taught first to provide language support. Commonly used and culturally appropriate word combinations can be discussed as a fun language-learning activity. ELLs can contribute by sharing different or similar word combinations from their native language to enhance understanding and language awareness.

Commonly used word clusters—especially those word collocations such as *verb + noun, adjective + noun, verb + adverb*, etc.—can be introduced purposefully before each writing or revision exercise. Everyday English words such as *take, make,* or *do* have the most combinations, as seen here (Tables 7 and 8).

## Table 7: Basic Word Collocations

| Make | Give | Have | Do | Take |
|------|------|------|------|------|
| Make an effort | Give a response | Have a reaction | Do homework | Take a message |
| Make progress | Give an example | Have a diet | Do a project | Take an opportunity |
| Make a mistake | Give credit to | Have permission | Do a lesson | Take a chance |
| Make peace | Give preference to | Have a brainstorm | Do a job | Take a flight |
| Make change | Give a hard time | Have a dream | Do my best | Take a break |
| Make a mess | Give rise to | Have a coffee | Do business | Take a shower |
| Make a comment | Give a reason | Have a relationship | Do exercises | Take a seat |
| Make a decision | Give a hand | Have a say | Do a project | Take power |
| Make sweat | Give feedback | Have a goal | Do a task | Take effect |

## Table 8: Common Academic Word Collocations

| Causal | Comparison | Time sequence | Reference |
|--------|------------|---------------|-----------|
| Result in | On the one hand, on the other hand | During the time of | In relation to |
| Give rise to | In spite of the fact that | At the same time | In reference to |
| Bring about | In contrast to | At the end of | In the context of |
| Lead to | With respect to | At the beginning of | In terms of |
| As a result of | Consistent with | In the process of | With respect to |
| Due to | Different from | As soon as | According to |
| Because of | Even though | As long as | Considering that |
| Effect of | On the contrary | Since then | To the fact that |
| The reason for | Relationship between | By the time that | From the point of view of |

Returning to the American Dream metaphors found in Langston Hughes' poem that were discussed in Chapter 2, the teacher can ask the class to brainstorm dream-related expressions and include word collocations as they do.

| Positive | Negative |
| --- | --- |
| Pursue my American dream. | Give up my American dream. |
| Make my American dream come true. | Fail in my American dream. |
| Find my American dream. | Lose my American dream. |
| Achieve my American dream. | Let go of my American dream. |
| Pass on my American dream. | Forget my American dream. |
| Advance my American dream. | Delay/defer my American dream. |
| Celebrate my American dream. | Neglect my American dream. |
| Enjoy my American dream. | Endure my American dream. |

The side-by-side comparisons of *dream* can draw students' attention to not only collocations but also connotations of these expressions to further the understanding of what an American dream is all about and at the same time explore the functional uses of those expressions.

# Word Connotations

*Language...has created the word "loneliness"*
*to express the pain of being alone. And it has created*
*the word "solitude" to express the glory of being alone.*
—*Paul Tillich*

*Connotation* is a culturally specific image or feeling or attitude associated with a word. The connotation of a word often poses difficulty for ELLs because it is connected with the culture, which ELLs are still learning. Without an insider's knowledge about the culture, ELLs probably will fail to comprehend or understand the deeper feelings associated with the word meaning. For example, *sissy* is another word for *boy*, but it carries connotations of a timid, childish, or weak man.

Native English speakers are bombarded by media and popular culture which communicate and use connotations to persuade the public on a daily basis. As students progress through their academic careers, they learn those culturally associated images, feelings, and attitudes along with the words they learn over time.

This is even true for academic and discipline-specific words. For example, while the phrase *flip flop* can have a positive connotation in science when it refers to the scientific method used in research, it takes on a negative connotation in social studies because it refers to a reversal of a decision made earlier, a tactic that politicians often use to persuade and gain public support.

Unfortunately, word connotations are seldom taught explicitly. For instance, going back to the example discussed in Chapter 1, color terms carry very different connotations from culture to culture (Figure 30).

**Figure 30: Cross-cultural Concept Collage 3**

As Figure 31 shows, connotation is highly dependent on context and culture for meaning and can be quite far from the literal meaning of the word itself. The word *propaganda*, which often carries a negative connotation in many American history textbooks, holds only positive or neutral connotations in Chinese or Spanish. Therefore, when native Chinese or Spanish speakers learn the word, they must also learn its English connotation in order to understand its historical significance in World War II or its use in literature, such as George Orwell's *Animal Farm*.

Word connotation instruction should be explicit, intricately connected with the teaching of culture, and contextualized within the text and the history in which the word is situated. For example, Stubbs (1995) discussed connotation of *big* and *small* in English. He pointed out how the word *big* takes on more metaphorical meaning as in *Big Apple, Big Bang, Big Brother, big government, big mouth, big words*. In these expressions—besides the positive connotations such as in *Big Apple* and *Big Bang*—the word *big* in the rest of the expressions has the negative connotation of *boastful, too much, controlling*, etc.

Semantic scales, thermometers, and matrices can be used to convey the varied connotations of words that have the same or similar meanings. One semantic scale, designed by Croviz and Miller (2008), is labeled *positive* at one end and *negative* at the other. It can be used to differentiate connotations of a group of synonyms for deeper understanding.

After the teacher or the class identifies synonyms, students then work in small groups or pairs to place them on the thermometer. They justify their placement by consulting dictionaries and thesauruses and talking with each other. Then they present their choices to the class.

Students are encouraged to use pop culture to describe the cultural images or feelings depicted by the word and their use in those contexts. For example, after filling out the word thermometer for *tapestry* (see Figure 32), the teacher can initiate a class discussion on the terms. Questions can be asked to promote the discussion, such as why does *nurse* only refer to a female? What is the male counterpart? What does it tell about our society? What is the equivalent in your native language? Do you have a term to describe a male nurse? What does it mean to be a *spinster*? What kind of feeling and attitudes does the word provoke? What is the male equivalent? Why do we use the gender terms we use?

Alternatively, the teacher can highlight varied synonyms of the word and ask students to discover the culturally relevant images or feelings these words evoke and rank them from positive to negative.

**Word thermometers.** A word thermometer diagram (Barton, 2001) is designed to differentiate nuances of meaning between a group of synonyms or words with similar meanings and to teach the connotations of each word. Though the words may be similar in meaning, they may have totally opposite connotations ranging from positive to negative. Once the words are placed on a vocabulary thermometer, the teacher can engage students in researching and discussing the context of the use, connotation, evolution, and history of each word to further students' thinking. (Figure 31).

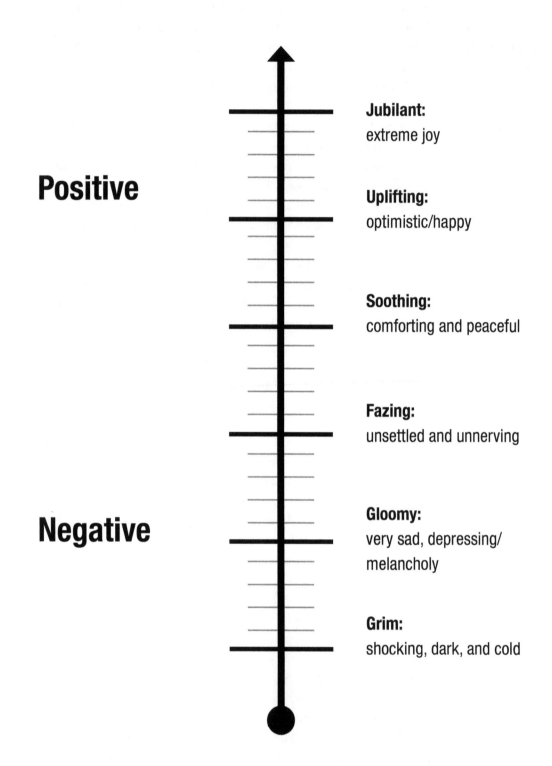

Positive

Negative

**Jubilant:**
extreme joy

**Uplifting:**
optimistic/happy

**Soothing:**
comforting and peaceful

**Fazing:**
unsettled and unnerving

**Gloomy:**
very sad, depressing/
melancholy

**Grim:**
shocking, dark, and cold

**Word tapestry.** A word tapestry refers to words that have virtually the same meaning but which depict very different images and complex feelings. Certain words lend themselves nicely to word tapestries, which can contain both pleasant and unpleasant feelings and images. Gardner (1998) described an exercise in which students filled in blanks with the equivalent of gender terms. They discussed these terms' connotations afterwards from social and cultural perspectives and questioned the assumptions held in a culture about female and male roles in society. By exploring the contexts in which these expressions are used and the evolution of these terms, ELLs learn both language and culture (Tables 9 and 10).

### Table 9: Gender Term Fill-ins

Fill in the following blanks with the equivalent female or male term.

| Female | Male | Female | Male |
|---|---|---|---|
| _____ | man | _____ | sissy |
| lady | _____ | chick | _____ |
| _____ | boy | _____ | king |
| Miss | _____ | bitch | _____ |
| _____ | sir | _____ | host |
| spinster | _____ | nurse | _____ |
| _____ | widower | _____ | wizard |
| shrew | _____ | bride | _____ |
| _____ | rapist | _____ | waiter |
| prostitute | _____ | maid | _____ |
| _____ | chairman | _____ | businessman |

### Table 10: Gender Term Connotations

Fill in the following blanks with the equivalent female or male term.

| Female | Male | Female | Male |
|--------|------|--------|------|
| woman | man | tomboy | sissy |
| lady | gentleman | chick | dude |
| girl | boy | queen | king |
| miss | mister | bitch | bastard |
| madame | sir | hostess | host |
| spinster | bachelor | nurse | nurse |
| widow | widower | witch | wizard |
| shrew | _____ | bride | groom |
| _____ | rapist | waitress | waiter |
| prostitute | pimp/gigolo | maid | butler |
| chairwoman | chairman | businesswoman | businessman |

# Euphemisms

Another way of exploring connotation is through euphemism, which is a more palatable choice to replace an offensive or negative word or phrase. Expressions, such as *friendly fire*, *collateral damage*, and *downsizing*, are used to replace hurtful and offensive ones. The expressions also are culturally specific in that they express certain thought processes, especially in business and political worlds. The teacher can ask the class to come up with and write on the board as many words as possible to describe, for example, the word *fat*. After listing the words, students can work in pairs or groups to match terms and respond to deeper questions, such as:

> What is the purpose of its use?
> How did the word/phrase evolve over time?
> What is the context of its use?
> Why is it necessary?

**Job title euphemisms**
Janitor: custodian

Garbage collector: sanitation worker

**Ability, economic, and physical euphemisms**
Remedial: developmentally disabled, has special needs

Poor: working class, of modest means, of humble origins, low income, unable to make ends meet, in debt

Fat: overweight, full figured, big boned, chubby, plump, voluptuous, portly

Handicapped: disabled, physically challenged, disadvantaged

### War euphemisms

Friendly fire: killing people on your own side

Soft targets: civilian targets

Collateral damage: dead civilians

### Death euphemisms

Bite the dust: die—often used for cowboys or desperadoes and suggests a violent end

Kick the bucket: die—reference to committing suicide through hanging by standing on a bucket and then kicking it away

Pass away/go to heaven: die

Final resting place: burial ground

# Word Structure

Many discipline-specific words are long words which can be cumbersome to comprehend and remember. In English, many words are created, however, from a limited number of roots, prefixes, and suffixes. Brown (1958) looked into *Webster's Collegiate Dictionary* and compiled a list of twenty commonly used prefixes and fourteen roots that generated 14,000 words! As students advance in their academic careers, they will encounter more and more words generated by these common word roots, prefixes, and suffixes.

Research has shown that knowledge about word structure is important for building independent vocabulary-learning habits and increasing word power. By learning these commonly used word roots and prefixes, students learn to look inside the word and develop skills for meaning-making in their reading. Paying attention to and explicitly teaching the structural characteristics of words pays great dividends as it supplies students with another tool for using morphological clues in reading and increasing word acquisition.

Instruction in word structure, such as creating and generating words derived from a specific root, also can be fun and exciting. For example, *bisect* can be read as *bi-sect. Bi-* is from the Latin *bi-*, meaning *two*, and *sect* is derived from the Indo-European root *sek*, meaning *to cut*. So *bisect* means *to cut into two equal parts*.

The prefix *bi-* can be found in many words, such as *biweekly, bipolar, bicycle, bilingual, binary, binomial, binoculars, bipartisan*, etc. Practice with roots, prefixes, and suffixes can expand students' vocabulary power and stimulate their interest and curiosity in language. Students will learn to view vocabulary not as a boring subject but as an intriguing, creative, and fascinating learning experience.

Many English words are derived from Romance languages, with Greek and Latin roots as two major sources for many words in biology, mathematics, chemistry, physics, history, and literature. Obviously, ELLs whose native languages are from the Romance language family have an advantage in learning words that share these roots. Having developed knowledge of their native language, these students can easily draw on their knowledge of word structure in their native language to understand English, thus speeding up the learning process. These students can be encouraged to help their peers understand the structure of those words.

On the other hand, ELLs whose native languages are non-Romance languages need more assistance in relating words to each other by their shared structure (morphology) and history (etymology).

Terry, a high school biology teacher, teaches a biology class consisting of all ELLs. She is big on promoting an understanding of scientific vocabulary, paying special attention to creating a rich context for learning scientific language. Learning through talking about the word structure is one context for teaching concept-based vocabulary for biology that is important in Terry's class. She constantly examines biology terminology from various angles, including a morphological angle. She uses that angle to approach certain words as shown here in an example of classification of organisms.

| | |
|---|---|
| Student 1: | I have a question for you. |
| Teacher: | Yes. |
| Student 1: | What's the difference between an autotroph and a heterotroph? |
| Teacher: | Terrific. What is the difference between an autotroph and a heterotroph? |
| | (Silence.) Look at the word. (Silence.) *Auto-* means what? Remember what we said about an automatic car. So *auto-* (writing on the board) means… |
| Student 3: | Itself. |
| Teacher: | Exactly. |
| Student 4: | My dad has an automatic car. |
| Teacher: | What makes it automatic? |
| Student 4: | It changes gears by itself. |
| Teacher: | Wonderful. That's why it's called *automatic*. So an autotroph is… |
| Student 4: | An organism that makes food by itself. |
| Teacher: | Yes, it makes its own food from raw materials. |
| Student 5: | We make our own food. |
| Teacher: | Well, we can make our own food. You can go into the kitchen and make your own food. But you can't make it from raw materials, like sunlight and water, and another word for *make* is *produce* (writes on the board)—produce food. That's the difference. Heterotrophs, like you and me and the rest of the animal kingdom, can't produce our own food. So how do we get food? |
| Student 4: | By hunting. |
| Teacher: | Hunting. How do you get your food (asking student 5)? |
| Student 5: | Cooking. |
| Teacher: | Hunting, cooking, growing, fishing, and going to Pathmark. But autotrophs can't pick themselves up and hunt, go fishing, or go to Pathmark. They have to find another way. So what is a heterotroph then? |
| Student 6: | A heterotroph is an organism that can't produce its own food. |

In Terry's classes, it was the norm for students to ask questions at the beginning of the lesson. As shown in the previous excerpt, when the student asks about the difference between an autotroph and a heterotroph, Terry engages the students in thinking about the morphological aspect of the language instead of just giving out the definition or assigning students to find out the meaning of the words in the dictionary. She offers real-life examples to create a rich context for thinking and meaning making.

Through active thinking, students discover the meaning for themselves. During the discussion, one student confuses humans as autotrophs because humans *make* their own food. Grasping that teachable moment, Terry introduces the key difference between the two by using synonyms and more examples to reconstruct new knowledge.

**"Root of the Day."** Vocabulary instruction using the word-structure strategy requires the teacher to examine discipline-specific vocabulary for common word roots and prefixes in subject-matter readings and discussions. "Root of the Day" (Bloodgood & Pacifici, 2004) is an activity that uses one word root as an instructional focal point. The teacher models and trains students to see how the word root can be spun into a map of cluster words. In the process, the class discusses word meanings and their changes, as well as the patterns in and logic of the varied combinations based on the root.

Roots may overlap among languages, thus teachers should encourage ELLs to share examples from their native languages during word root discussions. For example, Bloodgood & Pacifici (254) have shown that the prefix *poly-*, meaning *multiple*, can have numerous combinations as shown in the following word combination web (Figure 32).

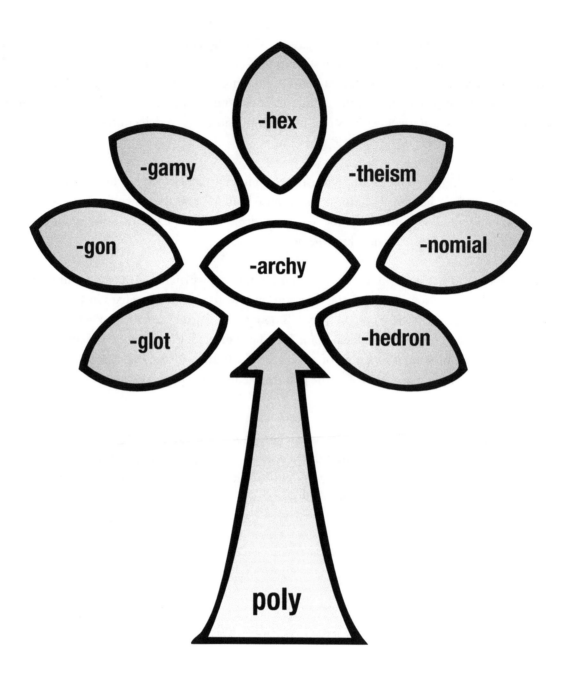

**Figure 32: Word Root Diagram**

Poly: multi
Polygon: multi-angle
Polyglot: multilingual
Polyarchy: a government run by many
Polygamy: multiple wives or husbands
Polynomial: multiple things or numbers
Polyhex: six angles
Polyhedron: multiple sides
Polytheism: multiple religions

# Contextual Clues

Guessing a word's meaning from its context is a widespread reading and vocabulary strategy used by good readers. It enables the reader to use contextual clues, knowledge of the topic, and word structure to reason and infer the meaning of the word without consulting a dictionary. Native English speakers have already established an oral language and basic vocabulary repertoire and are able to automatically look for these contextual clues to arrive at an appropriate meaning of the unknown word; ELLs have not. Word inference is valuable for ELLs because it enables them to learn vocabulary independently and speed up the process of reading, which enhances comprehension.

Research has shown that frequent pauses to look up an unknown word not only slows down reading but also distracts the reader from the main ideas and makes the reading experience frustrating. Using contextual clues to learn vocabulary helps minimize this need.

In order for the reader to infer a word's meaning correctly, however, several conditions have to be met. First, the reading material must present a favorable ratio of unknown to familiar words—about five to ten percent new words, with about one unknown word for every two lines is about right. With too many unknown words, the reader will be discouraged, and the chance of successfully inferring a word's meaning from its context declines (Hirsh & Nation, 1992). Once again, context-rich and appropriate language-level reading materials need to be included in the curriculum to provide opportunities and motivation for the reader to have success guessing a word's meaning from its context.

Careful selection of reading materials is especially important. Because the reading materials used for finding contextual clues must be language and reading level appropriate, the teacher can select children's picture books or even rewrite a reading passage to provide more contextual clues so that ELLs have enough familiarity with the materials to guess. The general guideline is to choose or rewrite the reading so that ELLs know ninety-five percent of the words and have sufficient context clues to guess the meaning of the remaining five percent of unknown words. Choosing an appropriate reading level ensures that the ELL will be focusing on *inferring* instead of *deciphering* meaning.

Also, instead of simply assigning the reading, the teacher needs to model the correct process and show how the inference starts, progresses, and arrives at a new meaning with a read-aloud and think-aloud activity. The teacher discusses all the important steps and clues in writing with students and reflects on their progress even after they have successfully guessed a word's meaning from its context. Since the strategy used for guessing the word from contextual clues is rather complex, the teacher needs to take time to let students practice one step at a time. Once students are fluent with the strategy, they will see the benefit and purpose of using it.

Another condition for successfully using contextual clues is that the reader must have good background knowledge about the subject matter on which the reading is based. That way, the reader can tap into his or her prior knowledge and actively relate and connect the reading topics with what is already known.

Next, students need to have some knowledge about word structures and be on the lookout for contextual clues as they read. For example, the word structure, punctuation use, and formation of the sentences are all relevant during the inference.

Finally, teachers need to model and train students with these strategies to build good habits of using contextual clues for reading comprehension and vocabulary learning. In addition, the teacher needs to integrate and measure the mastery of these skills into tests to assess and to motivate strategy use. For example, instead of only asking for definitions of a word on a test, the teacher may want to ask students to explain the strategies that they learned to guess word meaning from contextual clues on the test. That way, there is a consistency between instruction and assessment, and students can see the value of the vocabulary strategies they have learned.

When teaching subject-matter contextual clues to ELLs, some instructional adjustments should be made. Lacking word skills and years of English immersion, many ELLs have not developed solid oral language skills or do not know enough words to make complex inferences. Because they are new to the American academic culture, ELLs may not have the correct background knowledge about the subject matter they are reading. In other words, what they previously know may not help them guess correctly.

Second, in mainstream classes, ELLs often encounter reading messages far beyond their language and reading levels. When they are so confronted by a daunting number of new words in the reading, inferring is not going to be successful. In those situations, teachers need to either modify the reading or change the reading material.

Despite all the challenges, the benefits of using contextual clues to learn vocabulary far outweigh the drawbacks. After all, secondary ELLs who are learning English for academic purposes must develop competence in using contextual clues to learn vocabulary if they are to handle academic demands and become independent and active English-language users.

**Word contextual clue chart.** James, a ninth-grade English/social studies teacher, teaches in a block schedule. Students stay with him for both English and social studies classes for 90 minutes every other day. As an avid reader, he knows that guessing the word meaning from the context is an important strategy for reading and learning new vocabulary.

From his observations, however, James noticed that many of his non-native English-speaking students tend to over-rely on the dictionary and be reluctant to use contextual clues to guess unknown words. The ELLs would stop the reading frequently to find the meaning of the unknown word in the dictionary. Frequent interruptions during the reading compromised their reading speed, made the reading tedious, and hindered comprehension.

James decided to teach a unit on using contextual clues to unravel unknown words. He adapted five steps of guessing word meaning from context from Nations and Coady (1988) and engaged students to create a contextual word-learning journal entry. He introduced the students to four commonly used contextual clues that help them actively guess the word meaning in context.

- Example clues: The example before or after the word illustrates the meaning of the new word.
- Contrast clues: The opposite of the word meaning is given to ask the reader to deduce the meaning of the new word.
- Restatement clues: A definition or a synonym is given to show the meaning of the new word.
- Clues based on background knowledge: The reader is called to draw on his or her background knowledge associated with the new word to help with inferring its meaning.

James modeled these strategies one at a time for a week. He showed the class examples and gave handouts for students to practice. He also discussed their reading with the ESL teacher, who helped him assemble appropriate reading materials that paralleled his curriculum. He then asked his students fill out the Contextual Clue Log to monitor their independent word-learning habits (Table 11).

**Table 11: Word Contextual Clue Chart**

| Actual sentence in the text | Unknown word | My knowledge about the topic of the reading | Searching for contextual clues | My guess of the word meaning |
|---|---|---|---|---|
| | | | | |
| | | | | |
| | | | | |
| | | | | |

James found that once the reading passage was appropriate, students were able to let go of the dictionary from time to time so that they could focus on what they already knew instead of on what they did *not* know. Over time, students became fluent with these strategies and gradually changed from word "slaves" to word "detectives" (Table 12).

**Table 12: Deriving Word Meaning from Contextual Clues**

| Actual sentence in the text | Unknown word | My knowledge about the topic of the reading | Searching for contextual clues | My guess of the word meaning |
|---|---|---|---|---|
| The Egyptians also developed a form of writing, called hieroglyphics, that used pictures and symbols. From *World Cultures: A Global Mosaic*, p. 75. | Hieroglyphics | Not much. But I learned a little Egyptian history in the world history class back in my native country. I know Egyptians had a rich culture and history. | Definition/ explanation: The words before and after the new word helped me with guessing. They are: "a form of writing" and "that used pictures and symbols." | Hieroglyphics is a written language with pictures and symbols. |
| Confucius stressed this idea of filial piety, the duty and respect that children owe their parents. From *World Cultures: A Global Mosaic*, p. 331. | Filial piety | Being Chinese, I have learned about Confucius throughout my schooling back in China and my growing up. I think it must be something I've already known. | Definition/ explanation: The words after the new word helped me with guessing "the duty and respect that children owe their parents." | Filial piety is to show respect and listen to your parents at all times. |
| I often lied when I had to translate for her, the endless forms, instructions, notices from school, telephone calls. "Shemma yisz?"— What meaning?—she asked me... From *The Joy Luck Club*, p. 109. | "Shemma yisz?" | Again, as a Chinese, I can guess easily from the phonetic sounds. Also, the words before describe an experience that I often have when I translate something for my parents at the bank or doctor's office. | Punctuation/ restatement: The dash—right after the new phrase signaling the restating of the meaning of the phrase, "What meaning?" | What did they say? |
| Organisms, such as snakes and owls, that catch and eat other organisms are called predators. From *General Science*, p. 103. | Predators | I've learned some biology back in China. I know the words *snakes* and *owls*. | Definition/example: The examples given in the sentence, such as *snakes* and *owls*, and the definition of *organisms that eat other organisms* give away the meaning of *predators*. | Organisms that catch and eat other organisms. |

**Self-reflection during the reading.** In addition to using strategies of contextual clues, ELLs can also be asked to be conscious and reflective about their reading comprehension and vocabulary acquisition through reading. A series of self-reflective questions supports students as they search for contextual clues. Here is Harmon's (2002) list of self-reflective questions, which can be used with students as they search for the meaning of unknown words in reading.

What do you think the word means?

What makes you say that?

Are there other clues that made you think of that?

What is happening right here in the story?

What events are we reading about right here?

Why would the author use this word?

What does the word make you think of?

What do you notice about this word?

How did you figure that out?

What did you notice about what your partner said?

What strategies did you use?

What strategies did your partner use?

Were these strategies helpful?

Does the word meaning make sense?

By responding to those questions, students will be sensitive to how they read and begin to develop strategies to deal with unknown words. Here are a few helpful strategy statements that the teacher can talk about and model in class to show students how it can be done. These strategies are not limited to English class; all subject-matter teachers can teach these strategies for reading a textbook or comprehending test questions.

- I skip it and read on.
- I re-read it.
- I pause and think about what I'm reading.
- I sound out the unknown word to see if it is the word that I know.
- I look at the headings, the sentences before and after this word, and pictures for possible word meaning.
- I guess the meaning by looking at the parts of speech of the word.
- I break down the word into small parts to see whether I can recognize the structure of the word.

## Words with Multiple Meanings

English has many words with multiple meanings. As ELLs progress into secondary subject-matter classes, they find that many of the words they learned earlier take on different meanings. Sometimes those meanings are similar to the words' basic meaning and sometimes not.
Take the word *lens* for example. Students begin by learning that a lens is an optical device. As students move onto secondary schools, they will learn other meanings of the word as well. A lens is also the focusing device of the eye (biology), the structure behind the iris that focuses light on the retina (biology), a magnifying glass, a convex shape comprising two circular arcs joined at their endpoints (geometry), a curved transparent or translucent device that causes light to concentrate or diverge (physics), focus, and perspective (social studies and English).

When word meanings are as diverse as these, explicit teaching is necessary to not only add to students' vocabulary repertoire but also to distinguish the varied meanings and uses of the word in its context. In addition, some of these diverse meanings for *lens* may not be literal or concrete meanings anymore, but rather metaphorical, as in *critical-lens essays*, a term which refers to the use of high order-thinking skills to analyze and interpret two literary texts through a specific focus.

Words with multiple meanings post a special challenge for secondary ELLs. As they strive to catch up with their native English-speaking peers who have already acquired the basic meanings of many academic and discipline-specific words, they must acquire both the basic meaning of a word associated with sensory and concrete referents as well as the discipline-specific and metaphorical meanings.

Being aware of these students' backgrounds and needs, subject-matter teachers should be prepared to teach both the basic meaning and multiple meanings of the word as necessary—including metaphorical meanings.

Admittedly, that's a tall order. It is impossible to teach all the meanings of every single new word in class. It is possible, however, for subject-matter teachers to select and teach keywords that have multiple meanings—such as the word *civil*—which are used in varied contexts and carry different meanings in the subject matter under study, such as social studies in this case. (See the Suggested Resources for a recommended book to help teach words with multiple meanings.)

Teachers can ask students to accumulate a list of words used in their subject matter that have different meanings than their everyday meanings or that mean different things in different contexts or subjects. Students can chart the word like this.

**Table 13: Sample Words with Multiple Meanings across Subject-matter Areas**

| Word | Everyday meaning | Meaning 2 | Meaning 3 | Metaphorical meaning |
|---|---|---|---|---|
| Degree | Measurement of temperature or location | Measurement of an angle (mathematics) | A scale degree: the name of a note of a scale (music) | *To give someone the third degree:* to question sharply |
| Term | A time period, i.e., *semester* | Variable or expression (mathematics) | 4-year term limits: the 22nd Amendment of the U.S. Constitution that sets the limit for the President of the U.S. (social studies) | *On good/bad terms:* having a good/bad relationship |
| Lens | A device made of glass | Part of the eye (biology) | A shape comprising two circular arcs joined together (mathematics) | *Critical lens:* an essay about two pieces of literature |
| Period | Amount of time | Woman's monthly menstruation (science) | A punctuation mark (English) | *Grace period:* having extra time |

**Focused word study.** A focused word study brings students' attention to the meaning of a word as it appears in different contexts and changes its meaning and function depending on the context. It is an appropriate strategy to use after students have had repeated encounters in their reading with words with multiple meanings. The teacher can collect the words, with their multiple meanings and uses, and then present them the class. Students are asked to share their experiences with the words and guess the meanings when used in a context that the teacher presents.

Afterward, students are encouraged to create a collage or a chart of these meanings. They should organize varied meanings of one word according to its context, function, and disciplines. Here is an example of the illustration of the multiple meanings of *civil* (Figure 33).

### Figure 33: Multiple Meanings of Civil

| Civil service: service work for the government | Civil War: war between different parts within the nation; American Civil War was between the North and South from 1861 to 1865 | Civil ceremony: non-religious marriage ceremony to make the marriage legal | Civil manner: polite and courteous manner | Civil disobedience: non-violence and peaceful | Civil liberty: individual rights and freedom |
|---|---|---|---|---|---|
|  |  |  |  |  |  |

# Wordplay

As its name suggests, wordplay explores and conducts inquiries about a word under study in a playful way. By focusing on the playful power of language, the teacher brings fun and excitement into vocabulary instruction. Students like looking into language from a playful angle, and they develop an awareness of the rich language around them as well as a curiosity in discovering how language works.

Wordplay holds a special significance for ELLs who face tremendous challenges each day to read, speak, and write in English for different subject-matter classes. Wordplay actively engages their bilingual background to compare and contrast the two languages to promote associative and reflective learning. It provides a release from book-bound learning and gives ELLs a chance to experience their new language in a creative, authentic, and fun way.

**Word interviews.** A word interview allows students to question, respond to, explore, and interact with a new word—and in so doing, examine it in depth to make it their own. Word interviews can be used in all stages of vocabulary learning. Students first work in pairs or groups to respond to a series of questions about a word under study. They are encouraged to draw a picture if they like. In pairs, they then present their word to the class without saying the word. Instead, the pairs guide the rest of the class to make a series of inquiries about the word in question. Sample questions and clues are as follows:

What is your meaning in this context?
Draw an image of your word.
Who are your friends and enemies (synonyms and antonyms)?
How would you rank them (friends and enemies)?
Where are you from and how did you evolve over the years (etymology, root, prefix or suffix)?
Draw a picture of your history.
Who likes to use you most often and in what context?
How do you compare to other words (create a simile or metaphor using your word)?
What are your emotions and attitudes (connotations)?
What other words are you most likely to be with (collocation)?

A sample word interview looks like this (Figure 34).

### Figure 34: Word Interview with *Prohibition*

I'm a powerful word and used here to mean *banned, not being allowed to do something*. My friends are *forbid, disallow, veto,* and *censor*. My enemies are *allow, approve,* and *give consent to*. Among my friends, I'm ranked pretty top in terms of giving command against. To me, it can mean both good things and bad depending on the context. In our reading, it means something bad in that Sterling Brown is condemning the segregation and racial discrimination barriers that Whites set up for the Blacks when he writes:

Today they shout **prohibition** at you:
"Thou shalt not this,"
"Thou shalt not that,"
"Reserved for whites only"—
You laugh.

The online etymology dictionary shows that my word is formed by two parts: *pro + hibit*. Although the prefix *pro* often means *to move forward*, as in *proceed, produce, progress, project, promote*, etc., in this context, *pro* means *holding back*. This word can be used in many situations: in law, civil rights discussions, traffic, public areas, etc. by lawyers, judges, police, teachers, and people in authority.

To prohibit is closing doors.
Prohibition is like a dark cloud covering the horizon.
Prohibition is like not being allowed to open your Christmas gifts under the tree the night before.

*Prohibit* is often used with the word *from*. To me, this is a negative word indicating that you are doing something that you are not supposed to be doing—something illegal or unacceptable.

**Word hunt.** A word hunt explores and collects language that we use every day. It can focus on words used in a specific area of our daily life, such as commercials on weight-loss products, firefighters' jargon, sports jargon, or an intriguing word/concept that is used in a new and innovative way.

Students are asked to select a topic or area of interest to "hunt down" and collect related words by going into a mall, shopping center, drug store, or other location. Alternatively, they can interview firefighters or sports personnel or document words from TV commercials, websites, newspapers, the Internet, or magazines on the topic.

Unlike textbook vocabulary or teacher-selected words in handouts, a word hunt gives students ownership to explore words in their world and to put a personal stamp on their collections. Because it taps into their interests and hobbies, the word hunt is highly motivational.

Instead of an informal assignment based on everyday life, the word hunt can relate to academic vocabulary. Students can be assigned a list of academic vocabulary for which they find meaningful examples in the real world. If assigned in this way, students will

1) Create a list of words or phrases;
2) Cite their sources;
3) Show the exact context where the word was found; and
4) Discuss its meaning, connotation, and collocation.

They are also asked to notice any change, evolution, or invention of other words besides the words they collected and indicate the context and rationale for those changes. Students present their findings using visuals, such as a collage or PowerPoint slides. Following is an example of a PowerPoint presentation of 9/11-related words (Table 14).

**Table 14: Word Hunt Log**

| Word | Word definition | Word history | Word context and use | Connotation |
|------|-----------------|--------------|----------------------|-------------|
|      |                 |              |                      |             |
|      |                 |              |                      |             |
|      |                 |              |                      |             |
|      |                 |              |                      |             |

Norman, a social studies teacher, teaches a class of eleventh graders, with quite a few ELLs. When discussing current events, such as national security and terrorism, Norman noticed that his ELL students tended to be silent. His native English-speaking students used varied expressions and made several cultural references, using vocabulary that baffled his ELLs.

Talking with their ESL teachers during the lunch break, Norman realized that the vocabulary that he and his native English-speaking students used in class discussions was probably not yet part of his ELL students' linguistic repertoire. He also realized that his native English-speaking students, though fluent with those words, did not have an in-depth understanding of the underlying political and cultural circumstances surrounding these words.

Norman decided to create a group project on 9/11 language use. He invited students to gather expressions on themes of national security and terrorism from newspapers, magazines, and the Internet. Students were asked to list the definitions of these words and to also investigate the possible history and circumstances surrounding the creation or renewed interest in them.

Norman was pleasantly surprised to see his native English-speaking students and ELLs working together on this project. Some groups even came up with PowerPoint presentations to share their findings with the class. Here is an example of one presentation (Table 15).

## Table 15: Word Change since 9/11

| Word | Word definition | Word history | Word context and use | Connotation |
|------|-----------------|--------------|----------------------|-------------|
| Ground zero | The point at or directly above which a devastating event occurred (*Oxford English Dictionary*) | The word was originally used to describe the magnitude of the damage caused by the atomic bomb explosion in 1946. | The site of the former World Trade Center, once a huge pile of debris created by the collapse of the Twin Towers; the site of violent destruction and devastation provoked by evil doers | It has a negative connotation, conveying a sense of tragedy and destruction. |
| Sleeper, sleeper cell | A person who sleeps or is dormant before being activated (*Oxford English Dictionary*) | It was originally used as a scientific term, standing for "bacteria cells that communicate when chemically triggered" (Jack Rosenthal, 26). | Al Qaeda group sent out by their leaders to the U.S.; remained sleepers in the sleeper cells for a long time before they found a chance to strike. | It has a negative connotation, often referring to our enemies. |
| Regime change | A change of government peacefully from within (*Oxford English Dictionary*) | A regime normally has a negative connotation meaning *a government that people do not like.* It brought about the French Revolution when the old regime was down and the new government was established. | The Iraqi regime change was not peaceful but was instead a military effort to overthrow Saddam Hussein It's also the Bush administration's efforts to encourage other governments to join us in the fight. | Its connotation depends on for whom it is used. When the U.S. military or politicians talk about regime change, it has a positive connotation, indicating a good change. |
| Shock and awe | The intensity and overwhelming power used by U.S. military air strikes against Saddam Hussein | The phrase was first used in a book entitled **Shock and Awe:** *Achieving Rapid Dominance* written by James Wade et al and published in 1996. It described the U.S. dropping the atomic bombs on Hiroshima during World War II. | Behind the shock and awe, there was a horror that war inflicts, and if the term were used by our enemies, we probably would call it terrorism. | The word has a negative connotation. It has a sense of tragedy and destruction and conveys a sad feeling. |

**Idiomatic wordplay.** Fascinated by American sports and intrigued by the idiomatic expressions that their teachers use in class, a group of ELLs collected a list of sports-related idiomatic expressions. Because an idiom's figurative meaning is often closely linked to the literal meaning, students get the benefit of learning both the idiom and its original meaning. Following are some idiom posters that these students created (Figures 35, 36, and 37).

**Figure 35: Sports Idiom Poster:** *Down to the Wire*

Down to the wire: Near the end

Origin: It is dated in the late nineteenth century when the horserace course had a stretching wire across the finish.

It later became known at other occasions, meaning "at the last minute."

My sentence: The basketball game was so close, and we could not tell which team won down to the wire.

**Figure 36: Sports Idiom Poster:** *Throw in the Towel*

Throw in the towel: Give up

Origin: Its use began in boxing when throwing in the sponge and then towel meant the conclusion of a fight. It often is interpreted as a signal of defeat.

Later the idiom was used more widely to mean "giving up."

My sentence: I told John not to throw in the towel yet because I think he has something exciting to offer as student president.

**Figure 37: Sports Idiom Poster:** *Slam Dunk*

Slam dunk: A very forceful move or to move forcefully and dramatically

Origin: It comes from basketball, when the player leaps up and throws the ball into the basket from above.

It can be traced back to the 1960s when the term became popular in business and politics to mean "a strong and dramatic move."

My sentence: The mathematics test is a slam dunk for me.

**Word story.** Many words we use have a history of semantic change over time that can be traced. It can be fascinating for all students to study and share this history (etymology) by telling a story about the word and making connections that link its history with its use today.

Many idiomatic expressions also are shaped by historical conventions. For example, the idiomatic expression *kick the bucket* can be traced to the story of a person who wanted to hang himself by standing on a bucket with his head in a slip noose and then kicking the bucket out from under him. Thus, *to kick the bucket* means *to die*. Using a word's history to learn vocabulary increases the appreciation for a word or idiom, and it makes learning vocabulary fun.

### Lukas's word storytelling

My word is *lothario*. Based on Merriam-Webster's website, a man whose chief interest is seducing women is called a *lothario*. The word comes from the play, *The Fair Penitent*, by Nicholas Rowe. In the play, Lothario's main interest is women. He is an attractive man but very coldhearted. He has targeted to seduce Celista, who is a cheating wife. There are many lotharios that I can think of in our media. My older sister Kassiana always watches "Gossip Girl." Chuck, who is very similar to the original Lothario from the play, is also a deceiving and seductive man. His main target is Blair. Chuck has a lot of money and seduces Blair with gifts. He also has had more than one girlfriend at a time. I am sure that I will start to notice more lotharios in our media now that I learned the word.

## Homophones and Homographs

### "Do You *Here* or *Hear* What I Hear?"

Words can be quite deceiving
I have found
Words can have a double meaning
And sometimes a double sound.

We have *there* and *their* and *here* and *hear*
Watch what you're choosing
If it's not very clear,
It can all be quite confusing!

Can you tell me, if the clerk keeps *records*
And a song the musician can *record*
How can I make sense of words
Like these that can't be ignored?

Although a lawyer yells
"I *contest!*"
It's in a *contest* of words, he tells
Where he is at his best

I must declare
As I try to glean each word
That some words of a pair
Are the strangest I've ever heard!

Learning more day by day
So many words I can now read
Yet sounds and meanings, I must say
Have not always agreed (98)

(Poem appeared in *Journal of Adolescent & Adult Literacy, 51* (2) (2007), 98-111 written by Jacobson, J., Lapp, D., & Flood, J. entitled "A seven-step instructional plan for teaching English-language learners to comprehend and use homonyms, homophones, and homographs" © (2007) by IRA.)

The previous poem illustrates the confusing aspect of homophones and homographs in English. Homophones are words that share the same pronunciation but have different spellings and meanings, such as *hear* and *here* or *write* and *right.* Homographs are words that share the same spelling but have different sounds and meanings, such as *bow,* pronounced as /bau/, meaning *a bending gesture to show respect* and *bow,* pronounced as /bou/, meaning *a ribbon or a curved wood used to shoot arrows.*

Homographs and homophones are difficult for every student, but especially for ELLs who are still learning the sound-print-meaning association of English words. Yet they offer teachers good opportunities to focus on the contextual meanings of words and make good use of language ambiguity, a circumstance not unique to English.

The Chinese language, for example, has a tremendous number of homophones. The sound of the word *hui,* for instance, can carry different meanings or be written differently. Depending on the context, *hui* can mean *dust, waving, splendid, recover, badge,* and more.

**Visualization.** Teachers should approach this aspect of language acquisition with an open and positive mind. Rather than correcting student errors without comment, teachers can do more with this fascinating aspect of language. For example, visualizing homographs and homophones engages students in creating mental images to enhance comprehension and understanding (Jacobson, et al., 2007). When used along with information about pronunciation and the parts of speech, visualization helps students highlight and discuss the differences with their peers. Following are examples of such a visualization technique in action (Figures 38 and 39).

**Figure 38: Visualizing Homophones**

What are homophones? Words that share the same sound but with different spellings and meanings.

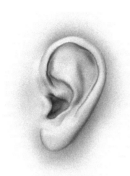

Hear /hɪr/
Verb
To listen with attention
*I hear the sound of music.*

Here
Adverb
In or at this place or point
*I'm here, and you are there.*

Hole /hoʊl/
Noun
An opening through something
*We dig a hole to plant our tree.*

Whole
Adjective
Having all parts
*I ate the whole pizza myself.*

Accept /ɪk'sɛpt/
Verb
To receive
*The winners will accept the trophy
at the award ceremony.*

Except vehicles displaying parking permit

Except
Preposition
With the exclusion of
*The main parking lot is closed to the public from
8 to 5 except vehicles with parking permits.*

## Figure 39: Visualizing Homographs

What are homographs? Words that share the same spelling but with different sounds and meanings.

Present /ˈpræzət/
Noun
A gift
*I received a big present on my
birthday from my parents.*

Present /prɪˈzɛnt/
Verb
To give
*I will present my paper to the class.*

Desert /ˈdɛzɜrt/
Noun
A dry sandy region with little rain
*New Mexico has a large desert.*

Desert /dɪˈzɜrt/
Verb
To leave and abandon
*"Don't desert me!" Jason cried,
begging his father to stay.*

bow /boʊ/
Noun
A curved piece of wood and a
string used to shoot arrows
*My uncle hunts wolves with arrows and a bow.*

bow /baʊ/
Verb
To bend at the waist to show respect
*The marshal arts students bow to their master.*

**Guessing game.** Another strategy that creatively teaches homophones or homographs is to use a guessing game in which students figure out the exact word from the context (see below). Students practice using homophones or homographs according to their meanings in the context. You can create your own little stories, or have the students create and exchange stories to correct.

(The words in parentheses are correct words.)

> Deer Jim,
>
> Hear (Here) I am in New York City. I've been hear (here) for too (two) weaks (weeks) now, and I can't bear (bare) the thought of going home. I'm in 9ᵗʰ grade this year. My English is getting a little better, but I still have a lot to learn and a lot to reed (read) and right (write) each day.
>
> In the photograph, you can sea (see) our apartment—its (it's) right next to the see (sea). The waves brake (break) on the beech (beach) just in front of our windows. Wan (When) it's moaning (morning) and it's stormy, the waves look like the manes and tales (tails) of white horses. It reminds me of home.
>
> I wish you could come and stay. The air fair (fare) is not that expensive. Hope to sea (see) you soon.
>
> Love,
> Jean

## Interactive Read-alouds and Think-alouds

There is a close relationship between reading and vocabulary development. The read-aloud, especially an interactive read-aloud where the teacher reads aloud and pauses to retell a story or the themes of the story, has shown tremendous benefits in motivating students to read, build on prior knowledge, and develop strategies to unlock both the meaning of a word and the process of reading itself. During the interactive read-aloud, the teacher stops to ask questions about the story line, themes, and characters; to explain difficult words; and to provide a rich context for language acquisition and vocabulary development.

In the process, the teacher also thinks aloud to show students how to use vocabulary-learning strategies to read effectively. The read-aloud that stops periodically when new words are encountered models the process by which students can monitor their own reading and thinking and supports the conscious use of strategies to facilitate reading comprehension. Moreover, many students have experienced sheer enjoyment through reading aloud with the whole class, listening as the teacher reads and makes observations about the story.

The idea of learning vocabulary through both reading and listening is especially helpful to students who are new language learners and who have difficulty with grade-level reading materials filled with new words and concepts. The teacher's interactive read-aloud develops prior knowledge and builds vocabulary. It also models pronunciation, which these students very much need but cannot get from silent, independent reading.

**The successful read-aloud.** The successful, interactive read-aloud that focuses on vocabulary development requires teachers to select reading materials and vocabulary carefully. Normally, the ideal read-aloud is a little above the readers' reading and language levels. A good read-aloud passage should include the following features:

- Interesting to students
- Relevant to the subject matter
- Written so that students can recognize and comprehend ninety percent of the vocabulary
- Containing one new word for every two or three lines
- Finished in about fifteen to twenty minutes' time

Here is a short list of possible readings that can be used for read-alouds in the subject-matter classroom (Table 16).

**Table 16: Subject-matter-specific Read-aloud Reading Materials**

| Title | Author | Subject |
|-------|--------|---------|
| The House on Mango Street | Sandra Cisneros (1984) | English |
| The Outsider | S. E. Hinton (2003) | English |
| Nighat | Elie Wiesel (1986) | English, social studies |
| The Diary of Ann Frank | Ann Frank (1942-1944) | English, social studies |
| The Constitution: Cornerstones of Freedom | Marilyn Prolman (1995) | Social studies |
| American History Poems | Bobbi Katz (1998) | Social studies |
| My Side of the Mountain | George Craighead (1959) | Earth science, life science |
| The New Way Things Work | David Macaulay & Neil Ardley (1999) | Physical science |
| Island of the Blue Dolphins | Scott O'Dell (1960) | Life science |
| Marie Curie and the Discovery of Radium | Ann Steinke (1987) | Biography, chemistry, physics |
| The Genius of Leonardo | Guido Visconti (2006) | Life science, physical science |
| Endangered Species | Christopher Lampton (2000) | Life science, environmental science |

Before reading, teachers should practice the reading beforehand for pauses and decide which word to explain and what questions to ask. It's wise to establish a clear purpose for the read-aloud, practice pronouncing difficult words to enhance engagement and enjoyment, and teach some specific reading skills and vocabulary-learning strategies.

Plan for students to participate with active listening activities, such as selecting new words. Prepare possible questions, and allow students to share responses, make connections, and voice confusions.

During the read-aloud, the teacher should always stop for questions and explanations. Finally, use follow-up reading and writing activities to extend the experience (Fisher, et al (2004) and Varela (2008)).

In their discussion of general guidelines for teaching vocabulary during read-alouds, Santoro, et al (2008) stated that selected words should be conceptual, be central to comprehending the meaning of the reading, and occur with high frequency in everyday communication and in academic language. Additionally, students should be encouraged to choose a few new words on their own from the same reading for further study or to use modeled reading strategies to guess their meaning.

John, a science teacher, established an interactive read-aloud routine early in the year in his sixth-grade science class composed of ELLs. Knowing that many of his students were at the beginning of language acquisition and had reading-comprehension difficulties, John spent a third of the time in class doing read-alouds of excerpts from the textbook.

He encouraged students to ask questions during and after each reading. The process of generating questions and discussing them, according to John, became a valuable part of the learning process. Here is an excerpt taken from a discussion after reading aloud from the textbook about the relationship between the environment and humans (Dong, 2005).

> Anna: What are gnus? They talk about gnus on this page, but I don't know what they are.
>
> Teacher: Let me read the paragraph. (A few minutes were devoted to John's read-aloud.) You're right, Anna. It talks about the lions eating the gnus, but what are gnus? Me being the teacher, I have no clue! Well, does anyone know what a gnu is?
>
> Maria: Maybe it's a small animal.
>
> Teacher: How small?
>
> Maria: (Shows about five inches in length)
>
> David: Maybe it's a lizard.
>
> Anna: Maybe it's in the picture on this page?
>
> Teacher: Maybe you are right. I don't know.
>
> Cynthia: Well, I think it's a big animal.
>
> Teacher: Why?
>
> Cynthia: Well, if we read the passage, it says that if these gnus were no longer living, then the lions would go hungry. Well, I know that lions are big animals, and so I think they must eat big animals. I think the lions would starve if they didn't eat big animals because they provide more food.
>
> Teacher: I think you have a point. Did everyone understand?

As shown in the above example, this part of John's interactive read-aloud is all about wondering about gnus, based on the context of the excerpt and the students' scientific thinking and literacy skills. Note that when students met an unknown word in the reading, John used it as a teachable moment to figure out the meaning of the word from the context instead of giving out the definition immediately. He invited students to look at the pictures, pose hypotheses, and ponder their own answers.

John's feedback is interesting. He responded, "Me being the teacher, I have no clue!" and "Maybe you are right. I don't know" when Anna basically asked for answers and confirmation. This issued an invitation for open discussion and interaction. In addition, acknowledging the student's question and echoing students' responses without an explicit evaluation places the students' voices at the center of the discussion, which sustains it.

# CHAPTER 5
## Teaching Vocabulary through Writing

• • • • •

*"When I use a word," Humpty Dumpty said in a rather scornful tone,*
*"it means just what I choose it to mean—neither more nor less."*
—*Lewis Carroll*

Writing plays an important role in subject-matter learning across all academic disciplines because it promotes thinking and learning about the subject and its vocabulary. Through writing, students clarify and organize their thinking, choose appropriate words to express their ideas and thoughts, and gain in-depth understanding of the words they learn. During the writing process, students have the opportunity to explore word meaning and apply the vocabulary that they learned for productive use.

In the subject areas, writing instruction generally focuses on organizing thoughts and clarifying ideas. How to use meaningful and lively vocabulary to pique reader interest or to extend the writer's ideas and thoughts on a topic are seldom considered. Using writing to teach vocabulary provides students with such a tool and provides the opportunity to experiment with new words in a creative, imaginative, and meaningful way.

ELLs with limited English vocabulary can find writing exercises to be difficult. They may not be able to find the appropriate or meaningful words that communicate their thoughts, even if their subject-matter skills are strong. Because their vocabularies are limited, ELLs' writing is often difficult to read, poorly organized, and lacking in grammar so that teachers have to puzzle through the writing to find meaning.

Even with these issues, however, a lack of adequate vocabulary emerges as the largest roadblock ELLs face as they try to express themselves as writers. Using writing to learn vocabulary gives these students extra time to think through their word choices and also provides ideas for their writing. Time for writing allows ELLs to practice making academic and discipline-specific words part of their repertoire. Applying vocabulary in writing actively engages students to interact with words at higher levels of thinking.

Various prewriting activities to support vocabulary and language instruction are especially necessary when working with ELLs. These include brainstorming with a word web, using a graphic organizer to organize thoughts, and furnishing students with a list of words to incorporate. Finally, explicit guidance about how to use resources, such as dictionaries and thesauruses, is needed, especially as support to incorporate advanced vocabulary.

Using writing to learn vocabulary requires two specific strategies: to purposefully build vocabulary requirements into the writing assignment and to center the writing assignment and writing processes around key vocabulary concepts. Teachers should encourage students to use newly learned words throughout the writing process to express their knowledge about the subject matter. During revision, for example, students can be asked to substitute more sophisticated vocabulary for words used in the draft.

To expand their vocabularies and apply the newly acquired words in writing, students should be encouraged during the drafting and revision process to use schematically related vocabulary, vocabulary closely related to the topic of writing, collocations of these words, and thesauruses. A few non-traditional exercises listed on the following pages are specifically designed to help students apply vocabulary to express themselves, as well as support deeper thinking about the concepts they are writing about.

## Some Non-traditional Writing Activities

**Haiku.** Writing haiku, brief and sensory poems about nature that originated in Japan, is a useful activity for ELLs. A typical haiku has these structural features:

First line: contains word(s) with five syllables
Second line: contains word(s) with seven syllables
Third line: contains word(s) with five syllables

Teachers can shift the focus of the haiku from nature to vocabulary concepts. For example, Sam, a fourth-year English teacher, introduced his poetry unit with haiku. Taking advantage of the class' recently completed Asian-American literature unit, Sam decided to move away from the routine and use a three-new-words-a-day approach to compose haiku. He first showed the class a few sample haiku he had found online and then modeled a couple of haiku. Then he asked the students to:

- Choose and focus on one word from their reading.
- Use the dictionaries to learn more about the word meaning.
- Draw the image based on that word meaning.
- Compose a haiku by following the structure.

The following is a sample of his students' haiku (Figure 40).

**Figure 40: Vocabulary Haiku**

Celestial sun
Keep shining your rays to bright
Kills the heinous night

**Word sensory poem.** A word sensory poem uses imaginative and figurative language to engage the writer's five senses. Words chosen for the sensory poems can be academic and discipline specific and need not be poetic. In fact, it is an even more rewarding and enlightening experience if students write about such a word using their imagination and creativity. The teacher can provide the class with something like this:

_____ is _____ (metaphor)

It looks like _____ (simile)

It sounds like _____ (simile)

It smells like _____ (simile)

It tastes like _____ (simile)

It feels like _____ (simile)

Using five senses to write a poem about a word requires students to go beyond ordinary and common definitions to discover unusual concepts behind the word. Developing similes and metaphors often requires the use of additional new words and further develops creative and critical-thinking skills. To compose a word sensory poem, students need to:

- Brainstorm words/ideas that center around the word in a word web;
- Change those words into similes that refer to the five senses;
- Use the word in the word web to complete the sensory grid;
- Write a simile for each sense (The teacher needs to show what a simile is and model how it is created using the word in the web as an example);
- Generate more words if necessary; and
- Create a metaphor for the poem (The teacher needs to show what a metaphor is, explain how it is different from the simile, and model one or two).

Sue, a pre-service social studies teacher, tutored a group of ninth-grade ELLs, who were learning world history in their social studies class. Sue used the sensory poem to teach commonly used words like *resource* and *conquer* that the ELLs needed help with, as well additional, grade-appropriate and discipline-specific words. With her help, students worked as a group to successfully compose poems like the following:

Resources sound like fresh, running spring water.
Resources smell like pine trees in the forest.
Resources taste like fresh produce in the supermarket.
Resources look like blue sky and burning sunshine.
Resources feel like money in our pockets.
Resources are the fruits of the earth.

Conquering feels like the joy after the battle.
Conquering tastes like sweet mango juice.
Conquering feels like a good rest after a long day.
Conquering looks like a bright light after a long dark night.
Conquering is a trophy after a tough match.
Conquering is to reach the highest mountain, standing tall and happy.

Using these figures of speech helped the students to think metaphorically and poetically. Such thinking helped the students create concrete and visual representations of abstract concepts, which in turn fostered concept understanding.

**Postcard writing.** Writing for real audiences and authentic purposes promotes concept and vocabulary learning. To explore key vocabulary in a general science class, Beth, a science teacher, assigned a postcard-writing activity to her eighth-grade class after she taught a unit on volcanoes. The card was designed to be given to the students' friends and family members, and it also served as an authentic assessment of subject-matter learning.

Students drew or downloaded a picture of a volcano, which they placed on one side of a 5" x 7" or 4" x 6" index card. They labeled the picture with at least five scientific terms. On the other side of the card, they wrote about the volcano using storytelling or description, incorporating science vocabulary into the picture and story.

Beth included volcanoes outside the United States to activate students' prior knowledge, provide a prompt, and to make the topic even more relevant to her ELLs. She found the list of active volcanoes through a Google search and marked their locations on the map that the site provided. She then divided students into groups of three or five by their nationalities or geographic regions. This way, students from the same countries and regions were able to work together on a volcano they might be familiar with. To help students use science vocabulary to talk about volcanoes, Beth posed a few questions before the activity began:

> What is your volcano?
> Where is it located?
> What causes it?
> What are the three main types of volcanoes?
> What are the major structures of a volcano?

Guidelines for the group postcards followed:

- Decide on five key volcano words that your group will choose to describe your volcano.
- On one side of your card, draw or download a volcano picture to illustrate the concept under study.
- Label volcano words you used on the picture.
- Tell a story about the volcano. Use the key volcano words on the other side of your card.

Students had fun with this activity because it extended their thinking about volcanoes and provided an opportunity for them to interact with words for an authentic purpose.

Here is an example of a word postcard (Figure 41).

**Figure 41: Word Postcard**

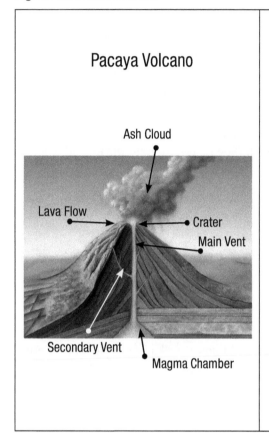

| | |
|---|---|
| **Pacaya Volcano**<br><br>Ash Cloud<br><br>Lava Flow — Crater<br>Main Vent<br><br>Secondary Vent<br>Magma Chamber | Dear Mary,<br><br>Last weekend, I visited Pacaya (see the picture on the left). It is an active volcano outside of Antigua Guatemala. It took me six hours to climb, and it was very, very hot. The ash cloud covered half of the sky.<br><br>On the left is a volcano picture for you to see. Magma is the very, very hot liquid rock that formed at the bottom of the volcano. When it is cooled down, it is called lava. The vent is the pathway that magma shoots up and flows out. At the mouth of this pathway, there is a crater that holds a pool of lava. In case the main vent is not working, the secondary vent will release the magma from the bottom.<br><br>But I enjoyed it because this time I was able to name some of the things I saw using the words I just learned in my science class, such as lava, cone, crater, etc. I wish you could have been there.<br><br>Your friend,<br>Yolanda |

**Word buffet.** Using a collection of sensory words, action words, and colorful adjectives to engage students in writing, a word buffet creates powerful images by combining the words creatively and critically. Students can work as a class, in groups, in pairs, or individually, searching for and gathering their words from a literature text or generating their own lists.

Teachers ask students to pick and choose the words they will need to compose a story, a poem, or an essay. The word buffet can be grouped according to genre, character descriptions, moods, actions, landscapes, perceptions, and more. Over time, students expand their vocabulary repertoires through purposefully collecting and using these words. As they write, students can refer back to and include words from their buffets.

Chris teaches eighth-grade English in a New York City school in which most students are ELLs. He just finished reading Gordon Park's poem, "Kansas." Many ELLs responded to it well, often comparing the poem with what they had experienced. Knowing that his students needed language support, Chris first invited the class to generate a collection of sensory words for a word buffet and put it on the board. The ELLs had a lot to say about their initial experiences in their new home city. Then Chris talked about the Park poem from a writer's perspective, noting important images that the poet created. Armed with the language, a model, and rich content, students worked in pairs to compose their own poems.

## Word Buffet for New York City

| See | Hear | Feel | Smell | Taste |
|-----|------|------|-------|-------|
| skyscrapers | traffic | seasons | fumes | bagels |
| yellow cabs | horns | weather | gasoline | pizza |
| people | sirens | heat | garbage | hot dogs |
| graffiti | languages | free | varied food | Chinese food |
| bridges | music | belonging | | |
| subway | | | | |
| stadiums | | | | |

New York City is full of cars and yellow cabs.

The horn sounds like bee, bee, bee!

New York City is full of birds and trees.

The birds on the trees are singing.

The trees envelope the city in a nice coat of green.

New York City is full of skyscrapers.

They are tall and crowded in Manhattan.

You see big advertisements on the buildings.

You hear loud music from huge TVs.

New York City is full of people—

Speaking different languages,

Eating different foods: pizza, hot dogs, and Chinese food.

It is the place where you feel you belong and are free.

**Writer's word palette.** The term *writer's word palette*, adapted from Noden's *image palette* (1999), can be viewed as a writer's tool in the same way that an artist's palette is used to create color. This prewriting activity helps students generate a collection of words and phrases that are relevant to the writing topic and group them into categories according to their function, organization, genre, etc.

The teacher first models the construction of a word palette using a passage from the textbook or literature. Then she asks the students to examine the writing of well-known writers to document how those authors use vocabulary and express themselves. With the model in mind, students purposefully collect words and phrases for their own writer's palettes as they encounter the words in their reading. Over time, this activity builds a repertoire of new words that prepares them for the subsequent writing assignment.

Sally, a ninth-grade biology teacher, teaches a mixed class composed of English language learners, newly mainstreamed ESL students, and native English speakers. Because the concept under study, *mitosis,* was complex and abstract, Sally designed a hands-on activity with construction paper to engage her students in visually and kinesthetically experiencing the mitosis process.

Students were asked to work in pairs, cutting construction paper to represent chromosomes and cells going through the process of mitosis. In preparing her writing assignment on mitosis, Sally first asked the ESL teacher in her school to help identify some language issues that might pose difficulty for her second language learners. She then came up with a writer's word palette to delineate specific language used to describe and understand the sequence of the mitosis process to provide language support for all her students in general and ELLs in particular. Below is such a palette (Table 17).

### Table 17: Writer's Word Palette on *Mitosis*

| Interphase | Prophase | Metaphase | Anaphase | Telophase |
|---|---|---|---|---|
| Mother chromosome<br>Father chromosome<br>Make copies<br>Replicate<br>Duplicate<br>Doubled | Daughter chromosome<br>Stick together<br>Come together<br>Combine<br>Condense | Move to the center<br>Line up | Separate<br>Divide | Move to opposite poles |

In the palette, Sally included both everyday words suggested by the ESL teacher, such as *stick together, make copies, move to the center,* and *separate,* as well as discipline-specific words, like *interphase* and *prophase.* She also included possible collocations, such as *mother chromosome, line up,* and *move to opposite poles.*

Once the students understood both the concept and the language, she asked each to write descriptions of what they just did sentence by sentence. Here is a sample English language learner's writing about the mitosis process (Dong, 2004/2005).

1. Cell grows to adult and gets ready to divide: Mitosis.

2. Father chromosome and mother chromosome come together. They make daughter chromosomes.

3. Daughter chromosomes stick together in center of cell.

4. They then separate and become two individual chromosomes.

5. They go to opposite sides of the cell.

With the help of Sally's table, students were able to combine their sentences into a paragraph using these scientific expressions. Here is the paragraph written by the same student based on the sentences above.

> When the father chromosome and the mother chromosome come together, they form a cell. They then go through the mitosis process. First, in interphase, each parent chromosome makes a copy of itself. Then during prophase the daughter chromosomes stick together and look like double chromosomes. Afterwards, these chromosomes go through metaphase as they move to the center of the cell and line up. They then go through anaphase in which they separate and become two individual chromosomes. Finally, these individual chromosomes move to opposite poles of the cell and the cell divides and goes through the mitosis process all over again.

**Writing petitions.** Jason, a pre-service social studies teacher, planned a lesson on the concept of *petition* to a class of eighth-grade ELLs. Because his students had come from diverse countries governed by different political systems, Jason was unsure that his ELLs had any idea about this concept. He prepared an example and asked his students first about the concept of *petition*. Even though many gave him blank stares, he did get a couple of responses.

Jason was relieved when a girl told the class "Yeah, I had to do that in my country. We all got together and signed a paper to the principal to stop bullying us." Since only a handful of students had some ideas about the concept of *petition*, however, Jason created a word web with the class to make the concept explicit and meaningful (Figure 42).

**Figure 42: Writer's Word Web on *Petition***

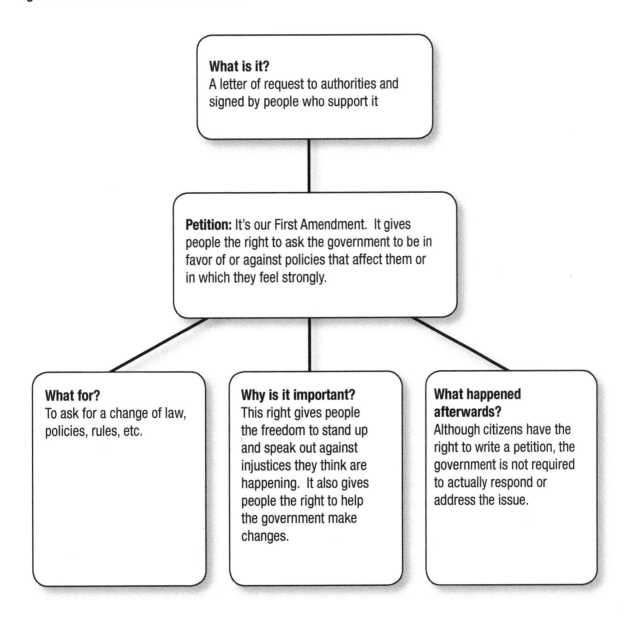

**What is it?**
A letter of request to authorities and signed by people who support it

**Petition:** It's our First Amendment. It gives people the right to ask the government to be in favor of or against policies that affect them or in which they feel strongly.

**What for?**
To ask for a change of law, policies, rules, etc.

**Why is it important?**
This right gives people the freedom to stand up and speak out against injustices they think are happening. It also gives people the right to help the government make changes.

**What happened afterwards?**
Although citizens have the right to write a petition, the government is not required to actually respond or address the issue.

After he was sure that the class understood the concept, Jason engaged his students in brainstorming petition topics and assigned a writing activity. The following are examples of students' writing.

Dear Dean,

I'm a student in 836 Class. I'm writing a petition about the seat arrangement in our school's cafeteria or lunchroom. I know that we have to behave during the lunch hour, and we cannot sit with our friends as we like. But I want to change this lunchroom rule because most people in the lunchroom are depressed. They want to sit with their friends and talk to their friends during lunch. I have my peers' signatures below to promise that we won't make trouble once the change is made.

Sincerely,
John


Dear Ms. Principal:

My name is Hanna from class 836. I admire you for watching this school. You are one of the brightest persons I've ever known and I can be sure to tell you just about anything.
I believe that most teachers only do things for the test not other important things. Testing ends on May 15. Social studies test is in June and is too hot to take it. Some kids are having a bad day in a hot day, so it's not fair. I think that you should change the state test day to do it each month. This year we are going to have a lot of tests, and we are going to be judged by one test like that. By having one test each month, we can have more time to study for just one test in a month before taking another one in another month. Thanks for your attention.

Sincerely,
Hanna


Dear Teacher:

I would like to make you a petition about no homework on Fridays and holidays. Everybody needs a free time after school and be out of worries and be with their families and friends. Without homework on Fridays we could have a weekend off and enjoy our weekends by playing sports and video games, going out with friends, and even visiting our relatives. If it is a holiday, I would like to be free also because the holiday is supposed to be without work. Employees are given holidays to enjoy, not to work. But we students have to study on holidays for upcoming tests. So I request you with all my due respect that I would like to have no homework on Friday policy. Please see below my peers signatures for their support.

Sincerely,
Ken Xin

**Word alternatives.** Word alternatives is a good revision activity. Students are invited to replace overused words, such as *nice, said, happy*, or *think*, with a synonym. As a whole-class activity, the teacher draws students' attention to these overly used words and conducts a mini-lesson on how to choose words that create vivid and interesting writing. Literature models can highlight specific examples of how writers replace common words with specific ones that make writing come alive.

Megan, a middle-school English teacher, pushes her students to use varied vocabulary to deepen their thoughts and create vivid imagery in writing. Although a few of her ELL students are still in the beginning stage of English language-proficiency levels, Megan puts a priority on expanding vocabularies in this way.

For example, after reading a story in which a student used the word *said* twelve times, Megan invited the class to generate as many words as possible to replace that word. She asked students to work in groups and to use dictionaries and thesauruses to find alternatives that fit the writing topic and context.

Megan then asked the whole class to look at the groups' writing and discuss the differences in writing that repeated the overused words too often with writing that replaced those words with fresh and specific choices. The following is an excerpt from their work.

> Sam stood outside the room where Mary and John were talking. He thought it sounded intimate and was curious to see what was going on between them. Before he entered the room he could hear what he thought sounded like an "I love you." But it couldn't be! He barged into the room and said (give another word for said) "What did you say?" Without even noticing Sam, Mary looked at John and said (give another word for said), "I love you." John said (give another word for said) back, "I love you." The three stood in silence after that moment as if time had frozen.

| Emotion | Instead of *said*, you say |
| --- | --- |
| Confused | question, inquire, request, query, ask, wonder, speculate, interrogate |
| Happy | declare, announce, compliment, cheer, affirm, applaud, hail, acclaim |
| Sad | cry, scream, sob, bellow, moan, groan, sigh, wail, grunt, whine |
| Angry | yell, shout, protest, bark, complain, demand, fuss, scold |

**Mathematical symbol translation.** Although mathematical symbols are universal, the expression of these symbols varies from language to language and thus often poses difficulty for ELLs. As students progress to secondary-level mathematics learning, they are not only required to know numbers and symbols but also to be conversant with the complex and abstract ideas behind these symbols. They need to be able to use the symbols to think, analyze, and express their thoughts in appropriate language.

A translation of the symbols into English reveals that mathematical symbols are deeper than labels alone; they are expressions of ideas and thoughts. For example, according to Usiskin (1996), putting $3x + 5 = 10$ into plain English should be as important for student understanding of the algebraic equation as the actual manipulation of the symbols and numbers.

Some symbols can be verbalized in multiple ways, such as X-*Y* (Rubenstein & Thompson, 2001). X-Y can be translated into:

- *x minus y*
- *x take away y*
- *x subtract y*
- *the difference between x and y*
- *x less y*

Translating those symbols into English poses a special challenge for ELLs, even though many come to the mathematics classroom with an advanced level of knowledge in the subject. They may not understand the concept behind or the relationship between the numbers they are working with. They may try to avoid the language aspect of mathematics learning, assuming that, as long as they can solve equations or problems, they should be fine.

Writing translations of mathematical symbols and then discussing them orally provides one way to support ELLs as they learn the concepts behind the symbols and gain competence in explaining them out loud. In this process, ELLs learn and practice varied language expressions and reflect on their understanding of mathematical symbols.

By bringing mathematical symbols to the center of the class discussion, the teacher can make all students aware of the concepts, help all students to clarify and deepen their thinking, enhance language acquisition, and correct misconceptions or misunderstandings. ELLs can be also asked to verbalize the symbols in their native languages and create a side-by-side comparison to enhance understanding of mathematical symbols in English (Tables 18 and 19).

**Table 18: Mathematical Geometry Symbols and Expressions**

| Symbol | Meaning | Example | Verbal expressions |
|---|---|---|---|
| o | Degrees | $\angle A = 60°$ | Angle A is sixty degrees |
| $\angle$ | angle | $\angle A = 45°$ | Angle A is forty-five degrees |
| ∟ | right angle | ∟ is 90° | A right angle is ninety degrees |
| $\triangle$ ABC | triangle | $\triangle ABC = \triangle EFG$ | Triangle ABC is equal to triangle EFG |
| \|\| | parallel | CD \|\| EF | Line CD is parallel to line EF |
| ∦ | not parallel | CD ∦ EF | Line CD is not parallel to line EF |
| $\perp$ | perpendicular | AB $\perp$ CD | Line AB is perpendicular to line CD |
| $\overline{AB}$ | line AB | $\overline{AB}$ | The line between A and B |
| $\overleftrightarrow{AB}$ | line AB | $\overleftrightarrow{AB}$ | The infinite line through A and B |
| $\overrightarrow{AB}$ | ray AB | $\overrightarrow{AB}$ | The line that starts at A and goes through B and continues on |
| $\cong$ | congruent | $\triangle ABC \cong \triangle EFG$ | Triangle ABC is congruent to triangle EFG |
| $\sim$ | similar | $\triangle ABC \sim \triangle EFG$ | Triangle ABC is similar to triangle EFG |
| $\therefore$ | therefore | $a = b \therefore b = a$ | a equals b, therefore b equals a |
| $\pi$ | pi | $\pi = C/2r$ | Pi is equal to the circumference divided by two times the radius |

## Table 19: Mathematical Algebra Symbols and Expressions

| Symbol | Meaning | Example | Verbal expressions |
|---|---|---|---|
| # | number | #54 | Number fifty-four |
| $\approx$ | approximately equal to | $a \approx b$ | a is approximately equal to b |
| + | addition sign, plus | $y + 9 = 15$ | A number increased by nine is fifteen |
| - | subtraction, minus, or negative | $x - y$ | x minus y<br>x take away y<br>x subtract y<br>the difference between x and y<br>x less y |
| x or $\cdot$ | multiplication | $a \cdot b$ | a times b or<br>b times a or<br>the multiplication of a by b |
| $\div$ or / | division | $a \div b$ | a divided by b or<br>b divides into a or<br>b divides a or<br>the division of a by b |
| $\pm$ | plus or minus | $x \pm y$ | x plus or minus y |
| $<$ | less than | $c < d$ | c is less than d or<br>d is greater than c |
| $\leq$ | less than or equal to | $x \leq y$ | x is less than or equal to y or<br>y is greater than or equal to x |
| $>$ | greater than | $a > b$ | a is greater than b or<br>b is less than a |
| $\geq$ | greater than or equal to | $a \geq b$ | a is greater than or equal to b or<br>b is less than or equal to a |
| $\neq$ | not equal | $c \neq d$ | c is not equal to d or<br>d is not equal to c |
| % | percent | 20% | Twenty percent |
| $|x|$ | absolute value of x | $|-3|=3$ | The absolute value of negative three equals three |
| ! | factorial | $5! = 120$ | The product of five times four, times three, times two, and times one is one hundred twenty. |
| $\sqrt{\phantom{x}}$ | square root | $\sqrt{4}$ | The square root of four or the positive square is four |
| $\sqrt[3]{\phantom{x}}$ | cube root | $\sqrt[3]{9}$ | Cube root of nine |
| ^ | exponent | $2^5 = 32$ | Two to the power of five is equal to thirty-two |

Sonia, an eighth-grade mathematics teacher teaching a class of ELLs, found out quickly that, although many of her students were quite proficient in mathematical symbols and calculations, they were silent when asked to volunteer their answers verbally. Many confided to her that they knew how to do calculations and arrive at the answer but did not know how to express those mathematical expressions in English. Sonia decided to set aside time during each class to teach students how to verbalize mathematical symbolic language in English.

One activity she designed was an interactive dialogue between the students through listening and speaking algebraic expressions. Sonia made multiple 4 x 6 index cards. On one side of each index card, she wrote an algebraic expression, and on the other side, she put the English translation of another algebraic expression. In class, she gave each student one card. Students listened carefully while one of their classmates read aloud the English translation on her card to see whether the expression matched the algebraic expression printed on their cards. Once the match was found, the matched student then read aloud the English translation on her card to see whose card had the matching algebraic expression. The activity continued until everyone had a chance to speak and find the match.

Below is a visual image demonstrating how this works (Figure 43).

**Figure 43: Interactive Mathematics Expression Dialogue Game**

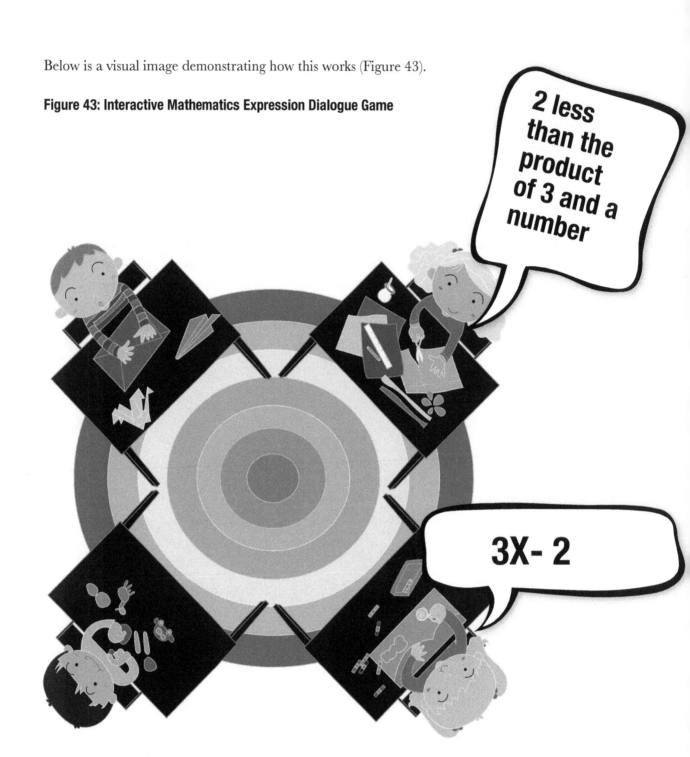

At the beginning of the activity, Sonia modeled the way to read aloud the English translation of an algebraic expression, asking students to pay close attention to the pause, intonation, and stress she used to decipher the subtle differences in algebraic expressions, such as *6 times…a number increased by 1*, which was translated into the algebraic expression *6(x+1)* and *6 times a number…increased by 1*, which was translated into *6x + 1*.

Throughout the exercise, students have to listen carefully and think mathematically to identify the match between the English translation and algebraic expression. They also have to speak up by reading aloud what is printed on their cards, thus practicing their English speaking skills.

**Rap and hip-hop lyrics.** Rap and hip-hop lyrics hold special appeal to ELLs in learning both subject-matter knowledge and vocabulary. The distinctive rhythm and oral poetry provide a rich context for learning vocabulary and pronunciation. Many secondary ELLs are fascinated by this part of American culture, and they are motivated to learn rap songs in order to fit in and be part of popular teen culture.

Even newly arrived ELL students gravitate toward music. Many listen to rap and hip-hop and talk about their music icons and stars with excitement. These musical genres provide ELLs with context-rich opportunities for vocabulary enrichment and practice for listening, pronunciation, and speaking. Students can even mimic lyrics to compose their own rap songs and, in the process, learn new words through reading, writing, listening, and speaking.

Flocabulary is rap lyrics specifically designed for vocabulary learning (Harrison & Rappaport, 2006). A group of rap artists use SAT vocabulary to compose these rap songs. They are conversational and filled with everyday vocabulary and rich metaphorical language to tell a story about the new SAT word. In the process, teachers can ask students to share their favorite rap artists and song lyrics with the class. Afterward, teachers either give the class a handout or show an overhead transparency of lyrics from Flocabulary for students to read silently or for the teacher to read aloud.

One good way to begin to teach rap and hip-hop is through a model such as one of the songs written by the Flocabulary. Next, the teacher can ask the class to go over the lyrics and talk about using rap lyrics to learn vocabulary. Then, the teacher asks students to work in groups, in pairs, or individually to compose their own rap lyrics based on the vocabulary under study. Guidelines include the following:

- Focus on the keyword and select varied words that share similar meanings with that word. Use the thesaurus to find synonyms.
- Write a story using your words.
- Create similes and metaphors for the words.
- Give rhyme structure to your lyrics by making two lines rhyme.
- Choose background music and create dance moves if necessary.
- Present your rap to the class.
- NO profanity or violence is allowed in your rap.

Lyrics also can teach concepts in subject-matter disciplines. The following is an example of rap lyrics composed by groups of ELLs and native English-speaking students.

## Superstition

You can find superstitions everywhere.
Some people believe in them,
Some people don't care.

When your palm itches,
You either get or spend money.
If you tell people that,
Some people might look at you funny.

It is a superstition that if your left eye jumps,
You're going to cry.
But the problem with superstitions
Is that you never know why.

Many West Indian cultures put a bible
Next to their baby's head when
They are sleeping because of tradition,
Some people do it because they think
It's superstition.

## Imperialism

Seizing is taking.
Manufacturing is making.
Britain seizes the opportunity,
Taking the poor nation's resources and exploiting their workers,
Making them sad and unhappy.
Imperialism gives power to the rich,
Making the poor nations their colonies.

# CONCLUDING REMARKS

• • • • •

L ike it or not, teaching vocabulary explicitly along with instruction about the concepts behind those words is now the job of all secondary teachers. Vocabulary should be at the heart of a subject-matter lesson, not at its periphery. Teaching subject matter effectively to ELLs requires moving beyond teaching new words in isolation with only a dictionary for support. Vocabulary lessons should be taught in context and with creative strategies that engage English language learners, who know too well how far behind they are and how much their success depends on learning academic vocabulary.

As those wonderful subject-matter teachers showed in the chapters of this book, effective instruction requires a long-term, systematic, and multi-dimensional approach. It includes drawing on ELLs' prior knowledge, connecting the word to multiple senses, and addressing the concept that the word represents in context. It requires students to interact with the word/concept at a deeper level through engaging reading, writing, talking, and thinking activities.

Because I am a second language learner myself, learning academic and discipline-specific vocabulary has been a long journey for me. I still remember the captivating tales about words told by my professors in graduate school and the exhilaration that I experienced when I used an idiomatic phrase properly. When ELLs share the same fascination and involvement with language as their teachers, the possibilities are endless.

It isn't easy to devote time to vocabulary instruction every day, to stimulate students' interest in and awareness of the language used around them, to share their word stories, or to explore how the word/concept contributes to learning the subject matter at hand. Yet, the effort is worth it. Listening, modeling, and training students in word-learning strategies will pay vast dividends in the lives of English language learners. It certainly made a difference in my life.

It is my hope that this book will provide you with the inspiration to reflect on ways to continuously improve your vocabulary instruction and give you the strategic tools to teach vocabulary effectively to English language learners. I wish you success in your efforts to make effective vocabulary learning happen in your classrooms.

# BIBLIOGRAPHY

• • • • •

Ainslie, D. (2001). Word detectives. *The Reading Teacher, 54* (4), 360-361.

Alexander-Smith, A. C. (2004). Feeling the rhythm of the critically conscious mind. *English Journal, 93* (3), 58-63.

Allen, J. (2007). Inside words: Tools for teaching vocabulary in grades 4-12. Portland, ME: Stenhouse Publishers.

Allen, J. (1999). *Words, words, words: Teaching vocabulary in grades 4-12*. Portland, ME: Stenhouse Publishers.

Antonacci, P. A. (1991). Students search for meaning in the text through semantic mapping. *Social Education, 55* (3), 174-175, 194.

Baart, N. (2002). Saying it more intensely: Using sensory experience to teach poetry writing. *English Journal, 91* (3), 98-103.

Bahns, J. (1993). Lexical collocations: A contrastive view. *ELT Journal, 47* (1), 56-63.

Barcrof, J. (2004). Second language vocabulary acquisition: A lexical input processing approach. *Foreign Language Annals, 37* (2), 200-208.

Barton, J. (2001). Teaching vocabulary in the literature classroom. *English Journal, 90* (4), 82-88.

Bauer, B. E., & Manyak, P. C. (2008). Creating language-rich instruction for English-language learners. *The Reading Teacher, 62* (2), 176-178.

Baumnn, J. F., Kame'Enui, E.J. (2004). Vocabulary instruction: Research and practice. New York, NY: The Guilford Press.

Bear, D. R., Helman, L., Templeton, S., Invernizzi, M., & Johnston, F. (2007). *Words their way with English learners: Word study for phonics, vocabulary, and spelling instruction.* Upper Saddle River, NJ: Pearson Prentice Hall.

Beck, I. L., McKeown, M. G., & Kucan, L. (2002). *Bringing words to life: Robust vocabulary instruction.* New York, NY: The Guilford Press.

Beers-Arthur, C., & Cook, B. (2008). Metaphorical graphic organizers, TESOL Annual Conference presentation.

Bialystok, E. (2008). *Learning a second language.* In A. S. Rosebery & B. Warren (Eds.) *Teaching science to English language learners: Building on students' strengths*, pp. 107-118. Arlington, VA: NSTA press.

Bittel, K., & Hernandez, D. (2006). *Kinesthetic writing of sorts. Science Scope, 29* (7), 37-39.

Gage, R. (1995). Excuse me, you're cramping my style: Kinesthetics for the classroom. *English Journal, 84* (8), 52-55.

Blachowicz, C., & Fisher, P. (2010). *Teaching vocabulary in all classrooms.* Boston, MA: Ally & Bacon.

Blachowicz, C., Fisher, P., Ogle, D., Watts-Taffe, S. (2006). Vocabulary: Questions from the classroom. *Reading Research Quarterly, 41* (4), 524-539.

Blasingame, J. Jr., Nilsen, A. P. (2005). The mouse that roared: Teaching vocabulary with source-based lessons. *English Journal, 94* (4), 59-64.

Bloodgood, J. W., & Pacifici, L. C. (2004). Bringing word study to intermediate classrooms. *The Reading Teacher, 58* (3), 250-263.

Boyer, T. L. (2006). Writing to learn in social studies. *The Social Studies, 97* (4), 158-160.

Brand, M. (2004). *Word savvy: Integrated vocabulary, spelling, & word study, grades 3-6.* Portland, ME: Stenhouse Publishers.

Braselton, S., & Decker, B. C. (1994). Using graphic organizers to improve the reading of mathematics. *The Reading Teacher, 48* (3), 276-281.

Bromley, K. (2007). Nine things every teacher should know about words and vocabulary instruction. *Journal of Adolescent & Adult Literacy, 50* (7), 528-587.

Bromley, K. (2002). *Stretching students' vocabulary: Best practice for building the rich vocabulary students need to achieve in reading, writing, and the content areas.* New York, NY: Scholastic Professional Books.

Brown, D. S. (2002). Creative concept mapping. *The Science Teacher, 69* (3), 58-61.

Bruna, K. R., Chamberlin, D., Lewis, H., & Ceballos, E. M. L. (2007). Teaching science to students from rural Mexico. *The Science Teacher, 74* (8), 36-40

Burke, J. (2003). *The English teacher's companion*, pp. 121. Portsmouth, NE: Heinemann.

Celik, M. (2003). Teaching vocabulary through code-mixing. *ELT Journal, 57* (4), 361-369.

Ciardiello, A. V. (2003). "To wander and wonder": Pathways to literacy and inquiry through question-finding. *Journal of Adolescent & Adult Literacy, 47* (3), 228-239.

Cobern, W. W., Gibson, A. T., & Underwood, S. A. (1995). Valuing scientific literacy. *The Science Teacher, 62* (9), 28-31.

Collier, V. P. (1989). How long? A synthesis of research on academic achievement in a second language. *TESOL Quarterly*, 21 (4), 617-641.

Connor, M. E. (1997). Teaching United States history thematically. *Social Education, 61* (4), 203-204.

Cooks, J. A. (2004). Writing for something: Essays, raps, and writing preferences. *English Journal, 94* (1), 72-76.

Crovitz, D., & Miller, J. A. (2008). Register and charge: using synonym maps to explore connotation. *English Journal, 97* (4), 49-55.

Cummins, J., Bismilla, V., Chow, P., Cohen, S., Giampapa, F., Leoni, L., Sandhu, P., & Sastri, P. (2005). Affirming identity in multilingual classrooms. *Educational Leadership, 63* (1), 38-43.

Cummins, J. (1984). Language proficiency, bilingualism, and academic achievement. In J. Cummins *Bilingualism and special education: Issues in assessment and pedagogy* (pp. 136-151). San Diego, CA: College-Hill.

Deignan, A., Gabrys, D., & Solska, A. (1997). Teaching English metaphors using cross-linguistic awareness-raising activities. *ELT Journal, 51* (4), 352-360.

Dong, Y. R. (2009). Linking to prior learning. *Educational Leadership, 66* (7), 26-31.

Dong, Y. R. (2009). www.ascd.org/ASCD/pdf/journals/ed_lead/el200904_dong_glossary.pdf

Dong, Y. R. (2006a). Tapping into the fund of knowledge that ELL students bring to our classrooms. *The NCTE Council Chronicle, 16* (2), 16.

Dong, Y. R. (2006b). Learning to think in English. *Educational Leadership, 64* (2): 22-27.

Dong, Y. R. (2004/2005). Getting at the content. *Educational Leadership, 62* (4), 14-19.

Dong, Y. R. (2004). *Teaching language and content to linguistically and culturally diverse students: Principles, ideas, and materials.* Greenwich, CN: Information Age Publishing.

Dong, Y. R. (2004). Don't keep them in the dark! Teaching metaphors to English language learners. *English Journal, 93* (4), 29-35.

Dong, Y. R. (2002). Integrating language and content: How three biology teachers work with non-English speaking students. *International Journal of Bilingual Education and Bilingualism, 5* (1), 40-57.

Egan, M. (1999). Reflections on effective use of graphic organizers. *Journal of Adolescent & Adult Literacy, 42* (8), 641-645.

Figgins, M. A., & Johnson, J. (2007). Wordplay: The poem's second language. *English Journal, 96* (3), 29-34.

Fisher, D., & Frey, N. (2008). *Word wise, content rich: Five essential steps to teaching academic vocabulary.* Portsmouth, NH: Heinemann.

Fisher, D., Flood, J., Lapp, D., & Frey, N. (2004). Interactive read-alouds: Is there a common set of implementation practices? *The Reading Teacher, 58* (1), 8-17.

Flynt, E. S., & Brozo, W. G. (2008). Developing academic language: Got words? *The Reading Teacher, 61* (6), 500-502.

Foil, C. R., & Alber, S. R. (2002). Fun and effective ways to build your students' vocabulary. *Intervention in School and Clinic, 37* (3), 131-139.

Folse, K. S. (2004). *Vocabulary myths: Applying second language research to classroom teaching.* Ann Arbor, MI: The University of Michigan Press.

Fontana, J. L, Scruggs, T., & Mastropieri, M. A. (2007). Mnemonic strategy instruction in inclusive secondary social studies classes. *Remedial and Special Education, 28* (6), 345-355.

Freeman, Y. S., & Freeman, D. E. (2009). *Academic language for English language learners and struggling readers.* Portsmouth, NH: Heinemann.

Fu, Z. Q. (2006). What to follow "make" and what to follow "do"—Corpus-based study on the de-lexical use of "make and "do" in native speakers' and Chinese students' writing. U.S.-China *Education Review, 3* (5), 42-46.

Gallavan, N. P., Kottler, E. (2007). Eight types of graphic organizers for empowering social studies students and teachers. *The Social Studies, 98* (3), 117-123.

Garcia, M. B., Geiser, L., McCawley, C., Nilsen, A. P., & Wo, E. (2007). Polysemy: A neglected concept in wordplay. *English Journal, 96* (3), 51-57.

Gardner, P. S. (1998). Out-looks and insights: A content-based unit on gender stereotyping. *College ESL, 8* (1), 70-82.

Garrison, D. (1990). Inductive strategies for teaching Spanish-English cognates. *Hispania, 73* (2), 508-512.

Genesee, F. (1995). ESL and classroom teacher collaborations: Building futures together. *TESOL Matters, 4* (6), 1-2.

Glomez, K., & Madda, C. (2005). Vocabulary instruction for ELL Latino students in the middle school science classroom. *Voices from the Middle. 13* (1), 42-47

Glynn, S. (1996). Teaching with analogies: Building on the science textbook. *The Reading Teacher, 49* (6), 490-492

Glynn, S. (1995). Conceptual bridges: Using analogies to explain scientific concepts. *The Science Teacher, 62* (9), 24-27

Goetz, W. W. (1993). Retrieving and reinforcing U.S. government using graphic organizers. *Social Education, 57* (2), 87-88.

Graves, M. (2007). Vocabulary instruction in the middle grades. *Voices from the Middle, 15* (1), 13-19.

Graves, M. (2006). *The vocabulary book: Learning and instruction.* New York, NY: Teachers College Press.

Graves, M. (1987). The role of instruction in fostering vocabulary development. In M. G. McKeown & M. E. Curtis (Eds.) *The nature of vocabulary acquisition* (pp. 165-184). Hillsdale, NJ: Erlbaum.

Gunderson, L. (2000). Voices of the teenage diasporas. *Journal of Adolescent & Adult Literacy, 43* (8), 692-706.

Hademenos, G., Heires, N., & Young, R. (2004). Teaching science to newcomers. *The Science Teacher, 71* (2), 27-31.

Harmon, J. M., & Hedrick, W. B. (2005). Research on vocabulary instruction in the content areas: Implications for struggling reader. *Reading & Writing Quarterly, 21* (3), 261-280.

Hecker, L. (1997). Walking, tinkertoys, and legos: Using movement and manipulatives to help students write. *English Journal, 86* (6), 46-52.

Hennings, D. G. (2000). Contextually relevant word study: Adolescent vocabulary development across the curriculum. *Journal of Adolescent & Adult Literacy, 44* (3), 268-279.

Hoelker, J. (2002). Scrabble with Latin and Greek roots and affixes. *TESOL Journal, 11* (2), 39-41.

Honnert, A. M., & Bozan, S. E. (2005). Summary frames: Language acquisition for special education and ELL students. *Science Activities, 42* (2), 19-29.

Howard, J. (2001). Graphic representations as tools for decision making. *Social Education, 65* (4), 220-223.

Howard, J. B. (1999). Using a social studies theme to conceptualize a problem. *The Social Studies,* 171-176.

Huckin, T., Haynes, M., & Coady, J. (1995). *Second language reading and vocabulary learning. Norwood,* NJ: Ablex Publishing Corporation.

Jacobson, Lapp, & Flood (2007). A seven-step instructional plan for teaching English-language learners to comprehend and use homonyms, homophones, and homographs. *Journal of Adolescent & Adult Literacy, 51* (2), 98-111.

Jameson, J. H. (1998). Simplifying the language of authentic materials. *TESOL Matters, 8* (3), 13.

Johnson, A. P., & Rasmussen, J. B. (1998). Classifying and super word web: Two strategies to improve productive vocabulary. *Journal of Adolescent & Adult Literacy, 42* (3), 204-207.

Johnson, D., & Steele, V. (1996). So many words, so little time: Helping college ESL learners acquire vocabulary-building strategies. *Journal of Adolescent & Adult Literacy, 39* (5), 348-367.

Kern, C., & Kent, J. C. (2008). Mapping for conceptual change: Concept mapping activities encourage students to develop scientific understanding. *The Science Teacher, 75* (6), 32-38

Kibby, M. (1995). The organization and teaching of things and the words that signify them. . *Journal of Adolescent & Adult Literacy, 39* (3), 208-223.

Kieffer, M. J., & Lesaux, N. K. (2007). Breaking down words to build meaning: Morphology, vocabulary, and reading comprehension in the urban classroom. *The Reading Teacher, 61* (2), 134-144.

Kleinheksel, K. A., & Summy, S. E. (2003). Enhancing student learning and social behavior through mnemonic strategies. *Teaching Exceptional Children, 36* (2), 30-35.

Klemp, R. M. (1994). Word storm: Connecting vocabulary to the student's database. *The Reading Teacher, 48* (3), 282.

Kopple, V., & William, J. (1995). Pun and games. *English Journal, 84* (1), 50-54.

Labbo, L. D., & Field, S. L. (1997). "Wish you were here!": Picture postcard explorations in children's books. *Social Studies and the Young Learner, 9* (4), 19-23.

Laframboise, K. L. (2000). Said webs: Remedy for tired words. *The Reading Teacher, 53* (7), 540-542.

Lakoff, G. (1993). The contemporary theory of metaphor. In Andrew Ortony (ed.) *Metaphor and thought,* pp. 202-251. New York, NY: Cambridge University Press.

Lakoff, George, and Mark Johnson. *Metaphors We Live by.* Chicago, IL: The University of Chicago Press, 1980.

Lamb, R. (2008). *Teaching vocabulary words with multiple meanings.* New York, NY: Scholastic Inc.

Lazar, G. (1996). Using figurative language to expand students' vocabulary. *ELT Journal, 50* (1), 43-51.

Lederer, R. (1991). *The miracle of language.* New York, NY: Pocket Books.

Levy, T. (1997). Postcards across America. *Social Education, 61* (5), 290-292.

Loughran, S. B. (2005). Thematic teaching in action. *Kappa Delta Pi Record, 41* (3), 112-117.

Low, G. (1988). On teaching metaphor. *Applied Linguistics, 9* (2), 125-147.

Manyak, P. C., & Bauer, E. B. (2009). English vocabulary instruction for English learners. The *Reading Teacher, 63* (2), 174-176.

Marzano, R. (2005). Direct vocabulary instruction: An idea whose time has come. In B. Williams (Ed.), *Closing the achievement gap: A vision for changing beliefs and practices* (2nd ed., pp. 48-67). Alexandria, VA: Association for Supervision and Curriculum Development.

Marzano, R. (2004). *Building background knowledge for academic achievement.* Alexandria, VA: ASCD.

Mastropieri, M. A., Scruggs, T. F., & Fulk, B. J. M. (1990). Teaching abstract vocabulary with the keyword method: Effects on recall and comprehension. *Journal of Learning Disabilities, 23* (2), 92-107. Metsala, J. L. & Glynn, S. (1996). Teaching with analogies: Building on the science textbook, *The Reading Teacher, 49* (6), 490-492.

McIntosh, M. E. (1994). Word roots in geometry. *The Mathematics Teacher, 87* (7), 510-515.

Meyers, L. M. (2000). Barriers to meaningful instruction for English learners. *Theory into Practice, 39* (4), 228-236.

Moen, C. B. (2007). Bringing words to life and into the lives of middle school students. *Voices from the Middle, 15* (1), 20-26

Moll, L. C., Amanti, C., Neff, D., & Gonzalez, N. (1992). Funds of knowledge for teaching: Using a qualitative approach to connect homes and classrooms.

Mountain, L. (2005). Rooting out meaning: More morphemic analysis for primary pupils. *The Reading Teacher, 58* (8), 742-749.

Nagy, W. E. (1988). *Teaching vocabulary to improve reading comprehension.* Urbana, IL: NCTE.

Nagy, W. E., & Anderson, R. C. (1984). How many words are there in printed school English? *Reading Research Quarterly, 21* (3), 304-329.

Nation, I. S. P. (2008). *Teaching vocabulary: Strategies and techniques.* Boston, MA: Heinle.

Nation, I. S. P. (2006). How large a vocabulary is needed for reading and listening? *The Canadian Modern Language Review, 63* (1), 59-82.

Nation, I.S.P. (1990). *Teaching & learning vocabulary.* Boston, MA: Heinle & Heinle Publishers.

Nelson, D. L. (2008). A context-based strategy for teaching vocabulary. *English Journal, 97* (4), 37.

Nesselhauf, N. (2003). The use of collocations by advanced learners of English and some implications for teaching. *Applied Linguistics, 24* (2), 223-242.

Nilsen, A. P., & Nilsen, D. L. F. (2004). *Vocabulary plus high school and up: A source-based approach.* Boston, MA: Pearson Education, Inc.

Nilsen, A. P., & Nilsen, D. L. F. (2003). A new spin on teaching vocabulary: A source-based approach. *The Reading Teacher, 56* (5), 436-441.

Noden, H. R. (1999). *Image grammar.* Pp. 13-15. Portsmouth, HN: Boynton/Cook.

Nokes, J. D. (2008). The observation/inference chart: Improving students' abilities to make inferences while reading nontraditional texts. *Journal of Adolescent & Adult Literacy, 51* (7), 538-548.

Ohanian, S. (2002). *The great word catalogue: FUNdamental activities for building vocabulary.* Portsmouth, NH: Heinemann.

Orgill, M., & Thomas, M. (2007). Analogies and the 5E model: Suggestions for using analogies in each phase of the 5E model. *The Science Teacher, 74* (1), 40-45.

Palmer, B. C., Shackelford, V. S., Miller, S. C., & Leclere, J. T. (2007). Bridging two worlds: Reading comprehension, figurative language instruction, and the English language learner. *Journal of Adolescent & Adult Literacy, 50* (4), 258-267.

Palmer, B. C., & Brooks, M. A. (2004). Reading until the cows come home: Figurative language and reading comprehension. *Journal of Adolescent & Adult Literacy, 47* (5), 370-379.

Paris, N. A., & Glynn, S. M. (2004). Elaborate analogies in science text: Tools for enhancing preservice teachers' knowledge and attitudes. *Contemporary Educational Psychology, 29* (2), 230-247.

Penick, J. E., Crow, L. W., & Bonnstetter, R. J. (1996). Questions are the answer. *The Science Teacher, 63* (1), 26-29.

Perrin, R. (2007). Words, words, words: Helping students discover the power of language. *English Journal, 96* (3), 36-39.

Pirie, B. (1995). Meaning through motion: Kinesthetic English. English Journal, 84 (8), 46-51.

Punch, M., & Robinson, M. (1992). Social studies vocabulary mnemonics. *Social Education, 56* (7), 402-403.

Rodriguez, T. A. (2001). From the known to the unknown: Using cognates to teach English to Spanish-speaking literates. *The Reading Teacher, 54* (8), 744-746.

Rosebery, A. S., & Warren, B. (2008). *Teaching science to English language learners: Building on students' strengths.* Arlington, VA: National Science Teachers Association.

Rosenbaum, C. (2001). A word map for middle school: A tool for effective vocabulary instruction. *Journal of Adolescent & Adult Literacy, 45* (1), 44-49.

Rubinstein-Avila, E. (2006). Connecting with Latino learners. *Educational Leadership, 63* (5), 38-43.

Rubenstein, R. N., & Thompson, D. R. (2001). Learning mathematical symbolism: Challenges and instructional strategies. *Mathematics Teacher, 94* (4), 265-271.

Rule, A. C., & Welch, G. (2008). Using object boxes to teach the form, function, and vocabulary of the parts of the human eye. *Science Activities, 45* (2), 13-22.

Salinas, C., Frenquiz, M. E., & Guberman, S. (2006). Introducing historical thinking to second language learners: Exploring what students know and what they want to know. *The Social Studies, 97* (5), 203-207.

Santoro, L. E., Chard, D. J., Howard, L., & Baker, S. K. (2008). Making the very most of classroom read-alouds to promote comprehension and vocabulary. *The Reading Teacher, 61* (5), 396-408.

Sassano, L. (2003). "I spy" engaged learners. *Voices from the Middle, 10* (4), 24-25.

Shanklin, N. (2007). What's this new emphasis on vocabulary all about? *Voices from the Middle, 15* (1), 52-53.

Seda, M. M., Liguori, O. Z., & Seda, C. M. (1999). Bridging literacy and social studies: Engaging prior knowledge through children's books. *TESOL Journal, 8* (3), 34-40.

Sekeres, D. C., & Gregg, M. Sr. (2008). The stealth approach: Geography and poetry. *Journal of Geography, 107,* 3-11.Simeone, W. F. (1995). Accommodating multiple intelligences in the English classroom. *English Journal, 84* (8), 60-62.

Sloan, M. S. (1996). Encouraging young students to use interesting words in their writing. *The Reading Teacher, 52* (3), 268-269.

Snow, C. (2008). What is the vocabulary of science? In A. S. Rosebery & B. Warren (Eds.) *Teaching science to English language learners: Building on students' strengths,* pp. 71-84. Arlington, VA: NSTA press.

Spencer, B. H., & Guillaume, A. M. (2006). Integrating curriculum through the learning cycle: Content-based reading and vocabulary instruction. *The Reading Teacher, 60* (3), 206-219.

Stahl, S. A., & Nagy, W. E. (2006). *Teaching word meanings.* Mahwah, NJ: Lawrence Erlbaum Associates, Publishers.

Stehr, L. S. (2008). Vocabulary size and the skills of listening, reading and writing. *Language Learning Journal, 36* (2), 139-152.

Strauch-Nelson, W. (2007). Magical words. *Art Education, 60* (4), 12-16.

Stubbs, M. (1995). Collocations and cultural connotations of common words. *Linguistics and Education, 7* (3), 379-390.

Svendson, A. (2002). Season it with Haiku. *TESOL Journal, 11* (1), 38-39.

Tatum, A. W. (2000). Breaking down barriers that disenfranchise African American adolescent readers in low-level tracks. *Journal of Adolescent & Adult Literacy, 44* (1), 52-64.

Taylor, D. B., Nichols, W. D., Rickelman, R. J., & Wood, K. D. (2009). Using explicit instruction to promote vocabulary learning for struggling readers. *Reading & Writing Quarterly, 25* (2), 205-220.

Templeton, S. (2003). Comprehending homophones, homographs, and homonyms. Voices from the Middle, 11 (1), 62-63.

Thornbury, S. (2002). *How to teach vocabulary*. England: Longman.

Tompkins, G. E., & Blanchfield, C. (2008). *Teaching vocabulary: 50 creative strategies, grades 6-12*. Upper Saddle River, NJ: Pearson Prentice Hall.

Uberti, H. Z., Scruggs, T. F., & Mastropieri, M. A. (2003). Keywords make the difference: Mnemonic instruction in inclusive classrooms. *Teaching Exceptional Children, 35* (3), 56-61.

Varela, A. (2008). Read-aloudshelpful in high school ESL classes. *Reading Today, April/May*, 21.

Wallace, C. (2007). Vocabulary: The key to teaching English language learners to read. *Reading Improvement, 44* (4), 189-193.

Weinstein, S. (2007). A love for the thing: The pleasure of rap as a literate practice. *Journal of Adolescent & Adult Literacy, 50* (4), 270-281.

Whitaker, S. (2008). Finding the joy of language in authentic wordplay. *English Journal, 97* (4), 45-48.

Whitaker, S. (2008). *Word play: Building vocabulary across texts and disciplines grades 6-12*. Portmouth, NH: Heinemann.

Wiggins, J., & Wiggins, R. (1997). *Music Educators Journal, 83* (4), 38-41.

Windschitl, M., & Buttemer, H. (2000). What should the inquiry experience be for the learner? *The American Biology Teacher, 62* (5), 346-350.

Winters, R. (2001). Teaching ideas: vocabulary anchors: Building conceptual connections with young readers. *The Reading Teacher, 54* (7), 659-662.

Wood, K. (2008). Mathematics through movement: An investigation of the links between kinesthetic and conceptual learning. *Australian Primary Mathematics classroom, 13* (1), 18-22.

Yopp, R. H. (2007). Word links: A strategy for developing word knowledge. *Voices from the Middle, 15* (1), 27-33.

Zareva, A., Schwanenflugel, P., & Nikolova, Y. (2005). Relationship between lexical competence and language proficiency. *Studies in Second Language Acquisition. 27* (4), 567-595.

Zimmerman, C. B. (1997). Do reading and interactive vocabulary instruction make a difference? An empirical study. *TESOL Quarterly, 31* (1), 121-140.

Zipke, M. (2008). Teaching metalinguistic awareness and reading comprehension with riddles. *The Reading Teacher, 62* (2), 128-137.

Zumwalt, M. (2003). Words of fortune. *The Reading Teacher, 56* (5), 439-441.

# SUGGESTED RESOURCES

· · · · ·

Ammer, C. (2001). *The facts on file dictionary of clichés.* New York, NY: Checkmark Books.

Benson, M., Benson, E., & Ilson, R. (1997). The *BBI dictionary of English word combinations.* Amsterdam, Netherland: John Benjamins Publishing Company.

Burchers, S., Burchers, M., & Burchers, B. (1998). Vocabulary cartoons. Punta Gorda, FL: New Monic Books.

Burchers, S., Burchers, M., & Burchers, B. (1997). Vocabulary cartoons: Building an educated vocabulary with visual mnemonics. Punta Gorda, FL: New Monic Books.

Burchers, S., Burchers, M., & Burchers, B. (2000). Vocabulary cartoons: Building an educated vocabulary with sight and sound memory aids. Punta Gorda, FL: New Monic Books.

Ehrlich, I. (1968). *Instant vocabulary.* New York, NY: Pocket Books.

Harrison, B., & Rappaport, A. (2006). *Flocabulary: The hip-hop approach to SAT-level vocabulary building.* Kennebunkport, ME: Cider Mill Press.

Lamb, R. (2008). *Teaching Vocabulary Words with Multiple Meanings.* New York, NY: Scholastic Teaching Resources.

*Longman essential activator* (1997). England, Pearson Education.

Makkai, A. (1987). *A dictionary of American idioms.* New York, NY: Barrons.

*Merriam Webster's vocabulary builder.* (1994). Springfield, MA: Merriam-Webster, Inc.

*Oxford ESL dictionary for students of American English.* (2000). Oxford, UK: Oxford University Press.

Resson, L. (1997). *A dictionary of homophones.* Hauppauge, NY: Barron's Educational Series, Inc.

Schwartzman, S. (1994). *The words of mathematics: An etymological dictionary of mathematical terms used in English.* Washington, DC: The Mathematics Association of America.

Skeart, W. W. (2005). *An etymological dictionary of the English language.* Mineola, NY: Dover Publications, Inc.

Spears, R. A. (1994). *NTC's dictionary of phrasal verbs and other idiomatic verbal phrases.* Lincolnwood, IL: National Textbook Company.

*The Newbury House dictionary of American English.* (1996). Boston, MA: Heinle & Heinle Publishers.

Titelman, G. (2000). *Random House dictionary of America's popular proverbs and sayings.* New York, NY: Random House.

## Translation Websites

http://freetranslation.paralink.com/
http://free.translated.net/
http://www.freetranslation.com/
http://www.free-translator.com/
http://babelfish.yahoo.com/

# APPENDICES

· · · · ·

## Appendix A: Secondary Academic Vocabulary

abbreviate
abstract
academic
access
accomplish
achieve
acquire
acronym
administer
advocate
affect
alter
ambiguity
analogy
analyze
annotate
anticipate
appeal
apply
appreciate
approach
appropriate
approximate
arbitrary
argue
assemble
articulate
aspect

assert
assess
assign
assist
associate
assume
assumption
attach
attitude
attribute
audience
authentic
aware

background
benefit
body
brainstorm
brief

calendar
calculate
cancel
capable
career
catalog
category
cause
challenge
characterize
chart

chapter
chronology
circulate
circumstance
citation
cite
claim
clarify
clue
coherent
colloquial
common
communicate
compare
compile
complement
complex
complicate
comply
component
compose
composition
conceive
concentrate
concept
concise
conclude
concrete
condition
conduct
configuration

confirm
conflict
conform
confront
consent
consequence
consider
consist
consistent
constant
constitute
construct
construe
consult
contact
context
continuum
contract
contradict
contrary
contrast
contribute
control
convey
cooperate
copy
correlate
correspond
create
credible
credit
crisis
criteria
critique
crucial
culture
cumulative

data
debate
decade
decline
dedicate
deduce
defend
defer

deficient
define
deliberate
demand
demonstrate
denote
dense
deny
depict
deprive
design
detect
determine
detrimental
develop
devise
deviate
devote
diagram
dictate
differentiate
diffuse
digest
dimension
direct
discourse
discover
discriminate
discipline
discuss
dispute
distinct
distinguish
distribute
diverge
diverse
doctrine
domestic
dominate
drama
drastic
duration
dynamic

economy
edit

effect
efficient
elaborate
element
elicit
eloquent
embody
embrace
emerge
emphasize
empirical
employ
enable
enhance
enlighten
enrich
ensure
entity
environment
episode
equal
equivalent
err
essay
essential
establish
estimate
evaluate
event
evidence
exaggerate
examine
example
excerpt
exclude
execute
exercise
exert
exhibit
expand
expert
explain
explicit
explore
expository
extract

fact
factor
facilitate
feasible
feature
figurative
figure
final
fluent
focus
footer
formulate
foster
fragment
frustrate
fulfill
function
fundamental

general
generate
genre
genuine
geography
goal
graph
gravity
guarantee

header
heading
hierarchy
highlight
homogeneous
hypothesis

identify
illustrate
imitate
imply
include
incorporate
indicate
indirect
individual
induce
infer

inferior
influence
inform
initial
initiate
innate
innovation
inquire
inspect
instance
instruct
integrate
intent
intention
interact
intermediate
interpret
interrogate
interval
interview
intrinsic
introduce
intuitive
investigate
invoke
involve
irony
irrelevant
isolate
issue
italics

journal
judge
justify

key

likely
label
laboratory
launch
layer
lecture
legislate
lens
liable

linguistic
list
literate
locate
logic

maintain
major
manifest
manipulate
margin
material
matrix
maximum
measure
medium
mental
metaphor
method
minimum
minor
model
modify
momentum
monitor
motive
myth

narrative
narrator
negative
network
neutral
norm
notate
novel
nutrient

objective
oblige
obtain
obvious
occupy
occur
odd
option

| | | |
|---|---|---|
| order | profile | result |
| organize | project | retell |
| orientate | prompt | reveal |
| origin | proofread | revise |
| outcome | propose | reverse |
| outline | prose | revolve |
| overlap | prove | rigid |
| | provoke | rigor |
| pace | publish | role |
| paraphrase | purpose | rotate |
| parenthesis | pursue | route |
| participate | | rudimentary |
| passage | quote | rule |
| passive | | |
| pattern | random | scan |
| perform | range | schedule |
| period | rank | score |
| perspective | rational | section |
| persuade | react | seek |
| phase | recall | segment |
| phenomena | reduce | select |
| philosophy | refer | semester |
| plagiarism | reflect | sequence |
| plan | reform | shift |
| plot | region | skim |
| point of view | regular | series |
| policy | reinforce | setting |
| potential | reject | show |
| portray | release | signal |
| possible | relevance | signify |
| precise | reluctant | significance |
| preclude | rely | site |
| predict | remove | sketch |
| prefix | render | solve |
| preliminary | rephrase | sophisticated |
| premise | report | source |
| prepare | represent | specific |
| prestige | reproduce | speculate |
| presume | request | spontaneous |
| preview | require | stance |
| previous | requisite | standard |
| principle | research | state |
| prior | resource | statistics |
| procedure | respond | stereotype |
| process | restore | strategy |
| product | restrict | structure |

study
style
subject
subsequent
substitute
subtle
succinct
suggest
sum
summarize
suggest
superficial
support
survey
switch
symbolize
synthesize

tangible
task
team
technique
temporary
tentative
term
terminology
test
text
theme
theory
thesis
timeline
tolerate
topic
trace
tradition
trait
transact
transfer
transform
transition
transmit
transparent
transport
trend
trial

trivial
typical

unique
utilize

vague
valid
variable
variation
vary
verbal
verify
version
viewpoint
vision
visual
voice
volume
voluntary

web
withdraw

# Appendix B: Secondary Biology Vocabulary

abdomen
abiotic
ABO blood group
abscisic acid
absolute dating
absorption
absorption spectrum
acetyl CoA
acid
Acquired
    Immunodeficiency
    Syndrome (AIDS)
Acrasiomycota
active immunity
active site
active transport
adaptation
adaptive
addition
adenine
Adenosine diphosphate (ADP)
Adenosine triphosphate (ATP)
adhesion
ADP (Adenosine diphosphate)
adrenal glands
aerobic respiration
aerosols
AIDS (Acquired
    Immunodeficiency
    Syndrome)
air sacs
algae
alimentary canal
allantois
alleles
allergy
alternation of generations
alveoli
amino
amino group
amniocentesis
amnion
amniotic fluid

amphibia
anaerobic respiration
anal pore
analogous structures
anaphase
anemia
angiosperms
Animalia
Annelida
anther
anterior
antheridium
anthropology
antibodies
anticodon
antigen
anus
aorta
appendicitis
appendicular skeleton
appendix
Arachnida
archaebacteria
archegonium
arteries
Arthropoda
Artiodactyla
Ascomycota
ascus
asexual
assimilation
asters
atomic number
atom
ATP (Adenosine triphosphate)
artia
atrioventricular (AV) node
auditory canal
auditory nerve
auricles
Australopithecus
autoimmune disease
automatic nervous system
autosomes
autotrophs
auxins

Aves
A-V node (atrioventricular
    node)
axial skeleton
axons

bacillus
bacteria
bacteriophages
ball-and-socket jockets
barbs
barbules
base
Basidiomycota
B-cells
behavior
benthos
bilateral symmetry
bile
binary fission
binomial
biodegradable
biogenesis
biology magnification
biology
biome
biosphere
biotic
bipedal locomotion
Bivalvia
blastocoel
blastopore
blastula
blue-green bacteria
bone
book lungs
Bowman's capsule
brain
brainstem
bronchi
bronchial tube
bronchiole
Bryophyta
budding
bulb

calorie
calyx
cambium
canals
cannies
capillaries
capillary action
capsid
carbohydrates
carbon fixation
carboxyl
Carnivora
carnivores
carrying capacity
cartilage
cast
catalyst
cell body
cell membrane
cell plate
cell wall
cells
cellular respiration
central nervous system (CNS)
centrifugation
centrioles
centromere
Cephalaspidomorphi
Cephalochordata
Cephalopoda
cephalothorax
cerebellum
cerebral cortex
cerebrum
cervix
Cestoda
Cetacea
chelicera
chemical bond
chemical formula
chemical reaction
chemoautotrophs
chemosynthesis
Chilopoda
Chiroptera
chitin

chlorophyll
chloroplasts
cholesterol
Chordata
chorion
chorionic villi sampling (CVS)
choroid coat
chromatin
chromatography
chromosomal mutation
chromosomes
Chrysophyta
chyme
cilia
Ciliophora
circadian rhythms
circulatory system
classes
cleavage
climax community
cloaca
clone
closed circulatory system
clotting
club mosses
cnidoblasts
cochlea
codominance
codon
Coelenterata
coelom
coenzymes
coevolution
Coleoptera
collagen
collar cells
colloidal dispersion
color blindness
commensalism
community
complement system
complete metamorphosis
compound leaf
compound microscope
compounds
concentration gradient

conditioning
cones
conifers
conjugation
connective tissue
consumers
contour farming
control
controlled experiment
convergent evolution
cork
cork cambium
corm
cornea
coronary
corpus callosum
corpus luteum
correlation
cortex
corticosteroids
cotyledon
covalent
cover crops
cranial nerves
cranium
Cro-Magnons
crop
crop rotation
crossover
crustacea
cuticle
Cyanobacteria
cycads
cytokinesis
cytokinin
cytoplasm
cytosine

dams
dark reactions
decomposers
dehydration synthesis
deletion
dendrites
denitrifying bacteria
deoxyribose

dermis
deserts
Deuteromycota
development
diabetes mellitus
diaphragm
diastole
diatomic
diatoms
dicots
differentiation
diffusion
digestion
dihybrid cross
Dinoflagellata
dipeptide
diploid
Diplopoda
Diptera
directional selection
disaccharides
disjunction
disruptive selection
DNA
dominance hierarchy
dominant
dominant species
dormancy
dorsal
double fertilization
Down syndrome

Echinodermata
ecological succession
ecology
ecosystem
ectoderm
ectothermic
Edentata
effector
ejaculation
electrons
electron transport chain
electrophoresis
element
elongation zone

embryo
embryo induction
embryo sac
endocrine glands
endocrine system
endocytosis
endoderm
endodermis
endoplasmic reticulum
endoskeleton
endosperm
endospore
endothermic
enhancer
entomology
enzymes
epicotyl
epidermis
epididymis
epiglottis
epinephrine
epithelial tissue
erosion
esophagus
estrogen
ethylene
Eubacteria
euglenoid
eukaryotic cells
Eustachian tube
eutrophication
evolution
excretion
exhalation
exocrine glands
exocytosis
exon
exoskeleton
external fertilization
extinct
extraembryonic membrane

$F_2$ (second filial generation)
facilitated diffusion
families
farsighted

fatty acid
feces
fermentation
ferns
fertilization
fertilizers
fetoscopy
fetus
fiber
filament
first filial ($F_1$) generation
flagella
flexor
follicle
food chain
food web
foot
foramen magnum
fossil
fossil record
fruit
fundamental tissues
fungi

gallbladder
gamete
gametogenesis
gametophyte
ganglion
gas exchange
gastric juice
Gastropoda
gastrovascular cavity
gastrula
gastrulation
gemmules
gene
gene mutation
gene pool
gene therapy
genetic drift
genetic engineering
genetic equilibrium
genetic recombination
genetics
genotype

geographic isolation
geologic evolution
geologic time scale
geotropism
germ layers
germ theory of disease
gestation
gibberellins
gill
gill slits
Ginkgo
gizzard
gland
gliding joint
glomerulus
glucagon
glycolysis
Golgi body
gonads
gradualism
grafting
gram-negative
gram-positive
gram stain
gram test
grana
grasslands
green-sulfur bacteria
growth
guanine
guard cells
gullet
guttation
gymnosperms

habit
habitat
habituation
haploid
Hardy-Weinberg law
Haversian canal
heart
helix
Hemiptera
hemocyanin
hemoglobin

hemophilia
hepatic portal
herbaceous stems
herbivores
heterotroph
heterotroph hypothesis
heterozygous
hinge joints
Hirudinea
histone
HIV (Human
      Immunodeficiency Virus)
homeostasis
homeotic genes
homologous structures
Homo sapiens
homozygous
hormones
horsetails
human ecology
humus
hybrids
hybrid vigor
hydrolysis
hydrotropism
Hymenoptera
hypersecretion
hypertonic solution
hyphae
hypocotyl
hyposecretion
hypothalamus
hypothesis
hypotonic solution

identical twins
immovable joint
immune response
immunity
implantation
imprinting
impulses
inbreeding
incisors
incomplete dominance
incomplete metamorphosis

index fossils
indicator
industrial melanism
inferior vena cava
inflammatory response
ingestion
inhalation
innate behavior
inorganic compounds
Insecta
insectivore
insight
instinct
insulin
intercellular
interferon
internal fertilization
interneuron
interphase
interspecific competition
intertidal zone
intestine
intraspecific competition
intron
inversion
invertebrate
in vitro fertilization
ion
ionic
iris
irritability
islets of Langerhans
isotonic solution
isotope

joint

Kaposi's sarcoma
karyotype
kidney
kilocalorie
kingdom
Koch's postulates
Kreb's cycle

labor
lacteals
Lagomorpha
large intestine
larva
larynx
lateral bud
lateral lines
law of conservation of mass
law of dominance
law of independent assortment
law of probability
law of segregation
layering
learned behavior
leaves
lens
lenticel
Lepidoptera
leucoplast
leukocyte
lichen
ligament
light microscope
light reactions
light system
limiting factor
linkage group
lipids
littoral zone
liver
lungs
lymph
lymphatic system
lymph node
lymphocyte
lysogenic cycle
lysosome
lytic cycle

macrophage
magnification
Malpighian tubules
Mammalia
mandibles
mantle

marrow
marsupial
mass number
maturation zone
mechanical system
medulla oblongata
medusa
meiosis
menstrual cycle
menstruation
meristematic tissue
meristematic zone
meristem
mesoderm
mesoglea
mesophyll
messenger RNA (mRNA)
metabolism
metamorphosis
metaphase
microdissection
microfilament
micropyle
mimicry
minerals
mitochondrion
mitosis
mixture
molars
mold
molecule
Mollusca
molting
Monera
monocot
monohybrid cross
monosaccharide
monotreme
morula
mosses
multiple-gene inheritance
muscle tissue
muscle tone
mutagen
mutation
mycelium

myelin
myofibril
Myxini
Myxomycota

nasal passage
nastic movement
natural selection
Neanderthals
nearsighted
nectar
negative feedback
nekton
nematocyst
Nematoda
nephron
nerve cord
nerve net
nerve
neuron
niche
nictitating
nitrifying bacteria
nitrogen fixation
nitrogen fixers
noise pollution
nomenclature
nondisjunction
nonrenewable natural resources
norepinephrine
notochord
nuclear envelope
nuclear acids
nucleoli
nucleotides
nucleus
nutrients
nutrition
nymphs

olfactory cells
omnivore
oncogene
one gene, one enzyme hypothesis
oogenesis
open circulatory system

operon
opposable thumb
optical system
optical nerve
oral groove
orders
organ
organelle
organic compound
organic evolution
organism
organ systems
osmosis
osmotic pressure
ossification
osteoarthritis
osteocyte
ovaries
oviduct
ovulation
ovule
oxidation
oxygen cycle
oxygen debt
ozone

pancreas
pancreatic juice
parapodia
parasite
parasitism
parasympathetic nervous
    system
parathyroid gland
parent generation
passive immunity
passive transport
pathogens
pedicle
pedigree chart
pedipalp
pellicle
pepsin
peptide
pericardium
penicillin

perichondrium
periosteum
peripheral nervous system
peristalsis
permafrost
petal
petiole
petrifaction
pH
phagocytic
phagocytosis
pharynx
phase-contrast microscope
phenotype
pheromone
phloem
photosynthesis
phylogeny
phylum
phytoplankton
pigment
pineal gland
Pinnipedia
pinocytosis
pistil
pith
pituitary gland
pivot joint
placenta
placental mammal
plankton
Plantae
planula
plasma
plasmid
plasmolysis
plastid
platelet
platyhelminthes
pleura
point mutation
polar molecule
pollen grain
pollen tube
pollination
pollution

polymer
polyp
polyploidy
polypeptide
pon
population
population genetics
pore
Porifera
positive feedback
posterior
precipitation
predator
pregnancy
premolar
pressure-flow theory
primary immune response
primary root
primary succession
primate
primitive gut
producer
progesterone
proglottid
prokaryotic cell
prophase
protein
proton
pulmonary artery
pulmonary circulation
pulse
punctured equilibrium
pupil
prostaglandin
pyramid biomass
pyramid of energy

race
radial symmetry
radicle
radiative dating
radioactivity
radioisotope
radula
range
reactant

receptacle
receptor
recessive
recombinant DNA
rectum
recycling
red blood cells
reduction
reflex
reforestation
regeneration
regulation
relative dating
releasing factors
renal artery
renal circulation
renal veil
renewable natural resource
reproductive isolation
Reptilia
resolution
respiration
respiratory pigment
restriction enzyme
retina
ribosome
RNA (ribonucleic acid)
rod
root cap
root hair
root
rumen
runner

saliva
salivary amylase
salivary gland
salt
saprobe
Sarcodina
saturated
scanning electron microscope
scavenger
Schwann cells
scientific law
scientific method

sclera
scrotum
secondary response
secondary root
secondary sex characteristic
secondary succession
secretin
secretion
sediment
sedimentary rock
seed
seed coat
selection
selectively permeable
semen
semicircular canal
sensory neuron
sepal
setae
sex chromosome
sex linkage
sexual reproduction
sickle cell disease
simple leaf
simple microscope
Sirenia
skeletal muscle
small intestine
smooth muscle
social behavior
sodium-potassium pump
somatic cell
somatic nervous system
species
sperm cell
spermatogenesis
spermatogonia
spherical symmetry
sphincter
spicule
spinal cord
spindle
spongy mesophyll
spore
sporophyte
Sporozoa

stabilizing selection
stamen
starch
stem
stigma
stimulus
stolon
stomach
stomate
strip cropping
stroma
structured formula
style
substrate
superior vena cava
suspension
sweat gland
symbiotic relationship
sympathetic nervous system
synapsis
synthesis
synthesis theory
systematic circulation
systole

T cell
tadpole
taiga
taste bud
taxonomic key
taxonomy
telophase
temperate forest biome
tendons
terminal bud
territory
test cross
testes
testosterone
theory
theory of evolution
thermal pollution
thigmotropism
thorax
threshold
thylakoid

thymine
thyroid gland
tissue
tracea
tracheal tubes
transcription
transduction
transfer RNAs (tRNAs)
transformation
translation
translocation
transpiration
transport
tropical rain forest
tropism
tundra
Turbellaria
tympanic membrane
typhlosole

ultrasound
umbilical cord
universal donor
universal recipient
unsaturated fat
urbanization
urea
ureter
urethra
urinary bladder
urinary
urine
uterus

vaccination
vaccine
vacuole
vagina
valve
variable
vascular bundle
vascular cambium
vascular cylinder
vas deferens
vegetative reproduction
vein

venation
ventral
ventricle
vertebrate
villi
virus
vitamin
vocal cord

warning coloration
water cycle
water-vascular system
white blood cell
windbreak
woody stem

X chromosome
xylem

Y chromosome
yolk sac

zoology
Zoomastigina
zooplankton
Zygomycota
zygospore
zygote

# Appendix C: Secondary English Language Arts Vocabulary

active voice
adjective
adventure novel
adverb
allegory
alliteration
allusion
apologue
antagonist
archetype
argument
autobiographical novel

blank verse
brainstorm
burlesque

canon
capitalization
character
characterization
citation
clustering
colon
comedy
coming-of-age story
comma
comma splice
composition
compound sentence
conflict
conjunction
connotation
convention

dangling modifier
dash
deconstruction
deductive reasoning
detective novel
dialect

dialogue
dictation
diction
draft
dramatic monologue

epic
epigram
essay
euphemism
exposition

fantasy novel
feminist criticism
fiction
figurative language
flashback
foreshadowing
found poem
free verse

genre
graphic novel

haiku
historical novel
humanism
hyperbole

independent clause
inductive reasoning
image
interjection
irony

limerick
literary convention
literary quality
lyric

Marxist criticism
mechanics
metaphor
meter
motif
multicultural novel

mystery novel
myth

narrative
narrator
new criticism
noun
novel

onomatopoeia
outline
oxymoron

parable
paradox
parallel
paraphrase
parody
passive voice
persona
personification
persuasion
picture poem
plagiarism
plot
point of view
preposition
prewriting
pronoun
proofreading
protagonist
pseudonym
psychoanalytic criticism
pun
punctuation

quotation

reader response
resolution
revision
rewriting
rhyme
romance
run-on

sarcasm
satire
scene
science-fiction novel
script
semicolon
sentence fragments
sequel
series
setting
simile
soliloquy
sonnet
speaker
stanza
style
subplot
suspense
symbol
syntax

theme
thesis
tone
tragedy
transition

Utopian novel

verb
verse
voice

Western
wordiness
writing process

# Appendix D: Secondary General Science Vocabulary

absolute zero
acceleration
accretion
acid
active metal
adaptation
air mass
animal kingdom
arteries
asteroids
astronomy
atmosphere
atom
atomic mass
atomic number

balanced equation
barometer
base
battery
Big Bang
binding energy
biome
black hole
blood
boiling point

capillary
catalyst
cell
cell membrane
cell wall
centripetal force
cerebellum
chain reaction
chemical equation
chemical formula
chemical reaction
chemical symbol
chlorophyll
chloroplast
chromosome
classification

climate
climax community
cold front
comet
community
complex machine
compound
concave lens
condensation
conduction
conductor
cone
constellation
consumer
continental rise
continental shelf
continental slope
controlled experiment
convection
convex lens
convex mirror
cosmic ray
covalent bond
crater
crest
critical mass
crust
crystal
cyclone

data
deciduous
decomposer
density
deposit
dew point
diaphragm
diffusion
digestion
DNA
dominant gene
dust

earthquake
eclipse
ecosystem

efficiency
electric circuit
electric current
electrode
electromagnet
electron
element
endangered species
energy
environment
erosion
esophagus
evaporation
evergreen forest
experiment
experimental factor
experimental group
extinct

fault
fertilization
focal length
focus
food chain
food pyramid
food web
force
force of gravity
fossils
frequency
friction
fungi
fusion

galaxy
gamete
gamma radiation
gas
gene
geologic map
glacier
greenhouse effect
grounding
group

habitat

halogens
heat
heat engine
heat of condensation
heat of vaporization
hibernation
hormone
hybrid trait
hydrocarbon
hydropower
hypothesis

igneous rock
impulse
indicator
induction
inertia
infrared radiation
inland sea
inner core
instinct
insulator
intensity
involuntary muscle
ion
ionic bond
isotherm
isotopes

jet stream
joint

kidney
kilogram
kinetic energy

lava
Law of Conservation of Energy
Law of Definite Proportions
lens
ligament
light year
liquid
liter
longitudinal wave
lunar eclipse

machine
magma
magnet
magnetic field
magnitude
mantle
mass
matter
medulla
meiosis
melting point
metals
metamorphic rock
mitosis
mixture
molecule
mutation

natural selection
negative change
neuron
neutralization
neutron
Newton's First Law of Motion
Newton's Second Law of Motion
Newton's Third Law of Motion
niche
noble gas
nonmetal
nuclear equation
nuclear fission
nuclear reactor
nucleus

observation
ocean front
opaque
organ
organic sediment
organism
outer core
oxidation
ozone layer

parallel circuit
period

periodic table
permafrost
pH scale
phases
photosynthesis
physical change
pioneer community
plane mirror
plant kingdom
plasma
polar molecule
pollination
population
positive change
potential energy
power
predators
pressure
prey
principle focus
producers
proton
pure trait

radiation
radioactive decay
radioactive nuclei
real image
recessive gene
reduction
reflection
reflex
refraction
relative humidity
renewable energy source
replicate
reproduction
resistance
respiration
revolution
rock cycle
rotation

S wave
salt
satellite

saturated zone
scientific law
scientific model
seas
sedimentary rocks
seismograph
series circuit
sex chromosomes
sex-linked trait
soil
solar eclipse
solar energy
solar system
solid
solubility
solution
sonar
specific heat
speed
spring tides
states of matter
static electricity
stimulus
stratosphere
structural formula
succession
sunspots
synapse
system

temperature
tendon
theory
tissue
topographic map
tracers
trachea
traits
translucent
transmutation
transparent
troposphere
trough
tundra

ultraviolet radiation
universe
urine

vascular plants
veins
velocity
virtual image
visual telescope
volcano
volts
volume
voluntary muscle

warm front
water table
watt
wavelength
weathering
weight
white dwarf
windward
work

zygote

# Appendix E: Secondary Mathematics Vocabulary

absolute value
acute angle
acute triangle
addition
addition property of equality
adding property
adjacent angles
algebraic denominator
algebraic expression
algebraic factorization
algebraic fraction
algorithm
alternate angle
altitude
angle
angle bisectors
area
associative property of addition
associative property of
    multiplication
asymmetry
average
axes
axis of symmetry

bar graph
base
basic counting principle
biconditional
binomial
bisect
bisector of an angle
bisector of a segment
binomial coefficient
binomial distribution
binomial theorem
bisectal circle
bisecting arcs
bisecting a shape

canceling
centimeter
chord

circle
circumference
coefficient
common factor
common multiple
commutative property of
    addition
commutative property of
    multiplication
complementary angles
composite number
conditionals
conditional equation
cone
congruent angles
congruent triangles
conjunct
consecutive integer
constant
coordinate axes
coordinate plane
coordinates
cosine of an angle
cube
cube root
cumulative frequency
    histograms
curves
cylinder

data collection
data organization
decagon
decimals
degree
denominator
depending events
diameter
digits
dilation
direct variation
discount
disjunction
distance
distributive property of
    multiplication

divisible
division property of equality
domain

equation
equilateral triangle
equivalent fractions
estimate
evaluate an expression
even number
event
expectation
exponent
exterior angle of a triangle

factorials
factors
factoring
fields
formula
fractions
frequency table

geometry
graph
gram
greatest common factor
grouping

hexagon
histogram
hypotenuse
hypothesis

identity element
independent events
indirect variations
inequality
inference
infinite
integers
interest
intersection of sets
inverse operations
inverse variations
irregular numbers

isosceles triangle

kilogram
kilometer

least common denominator
least common multiple
leg of a right triangle
like terms
linear equation
linear inequality
line
line graph
line reflection
line segment
liter
locus
logic
lowest terms

makeup
mathematical sentences
maximum
mean
median
meter
milliliter
millimeter
mixed number
mode
monomial
multiplication property of
    equality
multiplying by one property

natural numbers
negative number
null hypothesis
numerator
numerical expressions

obtuse angle
obtuse triangle
octagon
odd number
one-to-one correspondence

open sentence
operation
opposites
ordered pair
ordinate
origin
outcome

parabola
parallel lines
parallelogram
parentheses
pentagon
percent
percentile
perimeter
permutation
perpendicular lines
pi
placeholder
plane
plot
point
polygon
polynomial
positive number
postulate
powers
premise
prime factorization
prime number
principal
prism
probability
proof
proportion
protractor
pyramid
Pythagorean theorem

quadrant
quadratic equations
quadrilateral
quartiles
quotient

radicals
radius
random selection
range
rate
ratio
rational expressions
rational number
rational solutions
ray
real numbers
reciprocal
rectangle
rectangular prism
reflection
reflex angle
reflexive property
remote interior angles
repeating decimal
retail price
rhombus
right angle
right triangle
root
rotational symmetry
round number

sample space
sampling
scale drawing
scalene triangle
sets
scientific notation
segment
similar figures
similar polygons
similar triangles
simplest form
sine of an angle
slope
solution
solve an equation
space figure
sphere
square
square root of a number

statement
statistics
straight angles
substation method
subtraction
subtraction property of
    equality
supplementary angles
surface area
symbols
symmetric property of
    equality
symmetry
system of equation

table of square roots
tangent of an angle
term
terminating decimal
translation
transversal
tree diagram
triangular prism
trinomial
truth table
truth values
two-step equation

unlike terms

variable
vertex
vertical angles
volume

whole number
wholesale price

x-axis
x-coordinate
x-intercept

y-axis
y-coordinate
y-intercept

# Appendix F: Secondary U.S. History Vocabulary

abolitionist
abstract expressionism
administration
affirmative action
alien
allies
ambassador
amendment
American Exceptionalism
American Federation of Labor
anarchy
Anglo-Saxon
annex
antebellum
anti-federalists
anti-Semitism
antitrust
Appalachia
appeasement
arbitration
aristocracy
automation
Axis Powers

baby boom
balance of power
balance of trade
balanced budget
ballistic missile
bank holiday
Bank of the United States
belligerents
bill of attainder
Bill of Rights
bipartisan
Black Codes
black power
Black Tuesday
bloody shirt
brain trust
Brown v. Topeka Board of
     Education
budget
bureaucracy

cabinet
capital punishment
caravel
carpetbaggers
casualties
caucus
cautious revolutionaries
census
charter
check and balance
Chicano
citizen
civil liberties
civil rights
Civil Rights Act of 1964
civil service
clemency
Cold War
collective bargaining
colonization
colony
Columbian Exchange
commerce
Compromise of 1877
concentration camp
Coney Island
confederacy
congress
Constitution
containment
convention
convoy
coup d'état
currency

D-day
de facto
default
deficit
deflation
demilitarized zone
democracy
demography
deregulation
desegregation
détente
dictatorship
disarmament

discrimination
dividend
Divine Right Rule
domino theory
dust bowl

ecology
electoral college
Emancipation Proclamation
Embargo of 1807
embassy
emigrant
empire
Enlightenment
entitlements
ex post facto law
executive branch
exports

federal
federalism
Federalist Party
Federal Reserve System
filibuster
financier
foreclosure
Freedom Riders
Free Silver
frigate
Frontier

gag rule
G.I.
G.I Bill of Rights
Gilded Age
gold standard
GOP
grandfather clause
gross national product (GNP)
Great Migration

Hawks
head start
hemisphere
holding company
House of Burgesses
House of Representatives

immigrant
impeach
implied powers
imports
impound
impressment
imprisonment for debt
inaugurate
indentured servitude
indulgences
Industrial Revolution
inflation
initiative
injunction
interlocking directorates
international law
internment
interstate
iron curtain
isolationism

jazz
Jim Crow Laws
jingoism
joint stock company
judicial branch
Judiciary Act of 1801

Ku Klux Klan (KKK)

labor union
laissez-faire
lame duck
land-grant colleges
latitude
legal tender
legislation
legislative branch
lend-lease
literacy
lobby
lockout
longitude
loyalists
lynch

mainstreaming
majority
martial law
massive retaliation
master race
media
mediation
megalopolis
mercantilism
merchant marine
metropolitan
Middle Ages
Middle Passage
militarist
military-industrial complex
mollification
monopoly
muckrakers
mugwumps

nationalize
nativism
NATO
natural aristocracy
naturalism
naturalization
navigation system
neutrality
New Deal
New South
Nixon Doctrine
nonintercourse
nonpartisan
nuclear freeze
nuclear power

oil crisis
OPEC
ordinance
organized labor

pacifist
parallel
pardon
parity
Parliament

partisan
patronage
peculiar institution
per capita
petition
pioneers
plantation
plurality
Political Action Committee
    (PAC)
political machine
poll tax
popular sovereignty
pork barrel
preamble
precedent
president
productivity
Pearl Harbor
Prohibition
puppet government
ping-pong diplomacy
pragmatism
Progressive (Bull Moose) Party

quarantine
quota

racism
ratify
ration
rationalism
real income
reapportionment
recall
recession
reconstruction
red
redemptioner
referendum
refugee
regulation
Renaissance
reparations
representative government
republic

Republic Party
reservations
reverse discrimination
revolution
Right-to-work laws
rock and roll

salutary neglect
satellite nations
scalawags
secession
sectionalism
sedition
segregation
senate
seniority
separate but equal
separation of powers
settlement house
sharecroppers
shuttle diplomacy
sit-down strike
sit-in
social security
speakeasy
special interest groups
specie
speculator
sphere of influence
spoils system
stagflation
stalwarts
standard of living
staple crop
state's rights
status quo
stock
stockholder
Strategic Defense Initiative
strict construction
subpoena
subsidize
suburbs
suffrage
summit conference
superpower

supply-side economy
Supreme Court

tactical atomic weapons
tariff
temperance
tenant farmers
territory
third world
Tories
totalitarianism
treason
treaty
trust

ultimatum
unconditional surrender
unconstitutional
underground railroad
union
urban renewal
utopia

veto
Viet Cong

war criminals
welfare
Whigs
writ

yellow journalism
yellow press

# Appendix G: Secondary World History Vocabulary

abacus
abdicate
abolition movement
absolute monarch
absolution
Achaemenid dynasty
acid rain
acquired immune
    deficiency syndrome (AIDS)
acropolis
acupuncture
African diaspora
African National Congress
Afrikaans
Agora
agricultural revolution
ahimsa
Algerian National Liberation
Front
Allied Powers
American Anti-Slavery Society
Amnesty International
Amritsar Massacre
Angkor Wat
Anglo-Egyptian Treaty
animism
annex
Anti-Corn Law League
antibiotics
anti-Semitism
apartheid
apostolic succession
appeasement
aqueducts
archaeologist
armistice
aristocracy
artifacts
assembly line
astrolabe
Atlantic Charter
Atlantic Slave Trade
atomic bomb

atrocities
Auschwitz
autocracy
autonomy
Avesta
Awami League

baby boom
Babylonian captivity
balance of power
Balfour Declaration
Bantu languages
Bataan Death March
Battle of 'Ayn Jalut
Battle of Britain
Battle of Bulge
Battle of Lepanto
Bay of Pigs
Bedouins
Benedictine Rule
Berlin Conference
Berlin War
Bhakti
big bang theory
bilingual
Bill of Rights
biodiversity
bishop
Black Death
black market
blitz
Blitzkrieg
Bolsheviks
Boston Tea Party
Bourgeoisie
boxers
boycott
Brezhnev Doctrine
brinkmanship
bureaucracy
Bushido

caliphs
calligraphy
Calvinists
Camp David Accords

cantons
capital
capitalism
capitulations
captaincies
caravels
carbonari
Carlsbad Decrees
Carolingian Renaissance
Carter Doctrine
caste
Catholic Reformation
censors
Central Powers
Charter of Incorporation
Chartists
chinampas
chivalry
chlorofluorocarbon
Choson
Christian Humanism
chronometer
circumnavigate
citadel
city-states
civic humanism
civil disobedience
civilizations
civil service
classical education
Classic Maya
climate
Cold War
collective farms
collective security
College of Cardinals
colonus
Colossal style
command economy
Commercial Revolution
common law
Commonwealth of Nations
commune
communism
compass
compound bows

Concert of Europe
concordat
Concordat of Worms
Confederation
Congress of Vienna
conquistador
consensus
constitution
constitutional monarchy
consulate
consuls
consumption
Contadora principles
Continental System
contraband
Contras
Convention People Party
Coptic Church
corporation
Corpus Juris Civilis
cotton gin
Council of Trent
courtly love
covenant
covert
creole
crop rotation
crusaders
Cuban Missile Crisis
Cultural Revolution
culture
cuneiform
curriculum

D-day
Dada
daric
Dark Age
Darwinism
Dawes Plan
de-Stalinization
decipher
Declaration of Independence
decolonization
Delhi Sultanate
Delian League

demagogues
democracy
demography
demilitarize
demographic transition
dependent colonies
desertification
détente
devshirme
dharma
dialect
Diaspora
dictatorship
diffusion
dihqans
direct democracy
disciples
dissident
divan
diversification
divine faith
Divine Right of Kings
domain
Domesday Book
domestication
domestic system
dominion
domino theory
Donatary
Donation of Pepin
Dual Monarchy
Dutch West India Company
dynamo
dynasty

Easter Rising
Eastern Orthodox Church
ecosphere
Edict of Milan
Edict of Nantes
egalitarianism
elite
Elizabethan Age
Emancipation Proclamation
enclosures
encomienda

English Bill of Rights
enlightened despotism
entrepreneurs
Era of a Hundred Schools
Era of Warring States
Estates-General
ethnic cleansing
ethnicity
eunuchs
European Economic
    Community
European Union
Evangelical Movement
Exodus
exports
expressionism
extended family
extraterritoriality

fallout
Faqih
Fascism
Fashoda Crisis
February Revolution
Federal system
feudalism
fief
Fifth Republic
filial piety
financiers
fission
Five Classics
Five Pillars of Islam
flagellants
Flemish School
folk art
Forbidden City
formal logic
forum
Four Modernizations
Four Nobel Truths
Four Tigers
Fourteen Points
Fourth Republic
franchise
free enterprise

free trade
free world
freemen
French and Indian War
French Community
frescoes
fusion

Gang of Four
General Agreement on
    Tariffs and Trade
generation gap
genes
genocide
gentiles
geocentric
geoglyphs
geography
Ghazis
glasnost
Glorious Revolution
glyphs
globalization
global warming
Golden Bull
Good Emperors
Good Neighbor policy
Grand Canal
Great Bull Market
Great Chain of Being
Great Depression
Great Leap Forward
Great Migration
Great Schism
Great Trek
Green Revolution
greenhouse effect
griots
gross domestic product
guerrilla warfare
guilds
gulags
Guomindang
Gynaeceum

haiku
hajj
Hanseatic League
Harappan Civilization
Hawaiian League
hegemony
heliocentric
Hellenistic
Hermit kingdom
hieroglyphics
Hijrah
Ho Chi Minh Trail
holocaust
Holy Alliance
homelands
Homo sapiens
homogeneous society
hoplites
hubris
Huguenots
Hundred Days
Hundred Years' War

ICBMs
Ice Age
icon
Iconoclast Movement
ideograph
imams
Imperial Conferences
Imperial preference
imperialism
import substitution
indentured servant
Indian Mutiny
Indian National Congress
indulgences
Industrial Revolution
industrialization
infant mortality
inflation
Information Revolution
inquisition
Institutional Revolutionary  Party
integrated circuits
intendancy

interdependency
internal combustion engine
international debt crisis
Internet
intifada
Irish Revolutionary Army
Iron Curtain
Iroquois League
Islamic fundamentalism
Islamic resurgence
island-hopping
isolationism

Janissaries
jati
Jesuits
jihad
joint-stock companies
Junkers
junta

Ka'bah
kaiser
kamikaze
karma
kayaks
khan
Khmer Rouge
kiva
Kizilbash
Knesset
knights
Kristallnacht
Kulturkampf

La Noche Triste
laissez-faire
land reform
lasers
Lateen jail
Latin Christendom
latitude
Law of Return
legion
legitimacy
lend-lease

liberal arts
liberalism
lineage
Linear A
Linear B
Lobol
locomotive
loess
Long Court
Long March
longitude
lyric poetry

magical realism
Magna Carta
maize
mamluks
Mandarins
mandate
Mandate Heaven
maniples
manorial system
mansabdari system
Maoism
market economy
martyrs
Marxism
mau-mau
May Fourth Movement
means of production
Meiji Restoration
memsahibs
mercantilism
meritocracy
messiah
microscope
middle class
Middle Passage
militarism
millet
Ministry for International
    Trade and Industry
Missouri Compromise
mobilization
monasticism
monoculture

monopoly
monotheism
Monroe Doctrine
monsoons
mosaics
mosque
Mothers of the Plaza de Mayo
multiculturalism
mummification
Munich Conference
Murshid
Muslim Brotherhood
Muslim League
Mwene Mutapa
mystery religion

Nahuatl
Napoleonic Code
National Aeronautics and
    Space Administration
National Assembly
National self-determination
nationalism
NATO
natural law
natural selection
Navigation Acts
Nazi Party
Neutrality Acts
New Imperialism New Kingdom
nihilists
NKVD
nobles
nomads
Non-alignment
nonconformists
Norman Conquest
North American Free
    Trade Agreement
Northwest Passage
Nubian dynasty
nuclear family

oases
October Manifesto
oil embargo

Old Regime
oligarchy
on margin
open-field farming
Operation Barbarossa
Opium Wars
oracle bones
oral traditions
Organization of African Unity
Organization of American
    States
Organization of Petroleum
    Exporting Countries
ozone layer

pacifism
Padishah
Palestine Liberation
    Organization
Pan-Africanism
Pan-Arabism
Pan-Hellenism
Pan-Slavism
Panama Canal
pandemic
papyrus
parable
Parlement of Paris
Parliament
pastoralism
paterfamilias
Pathet Lao
patriarchal
patriachs
patricians
Pax Romana
Peace of Augsburg
peaceful coexistence
peninsular
pentarchy
people's communes
per capita income
perestroika
petro dollars
phalanx
pharaoph

philosophes

pictographs

plateu

Platt Amendment

plebeians

pogroms

polis

Polish corridor

polygamy

polytheistic

pope

popular sovereignty

population density

population explosion

praetors

predestination

prefects

proletariat

propaganda

protectionism

Protestant Reformation

Proto-Bantu

pueblos


Qanats

Quadruple Alliance

Quebec Act

Quechua

quipu

Qur'an

Quriltai


rabbis

racism

radar

radiocarbon dating

raj

raja

Ramayana

rationalism

realism

Realpolitik

Red Army

Red Guards

Red Scare

regionalism

reign of terror

reincarnation

Renaissance

reparations

reprisal

republic

resistance

responsible government

revolution

Revolution of 1905

rhetoric

Rigveda

Risorgimento

Romanticism

Roosevelt Corollary

Russification


Sacraments

salon

samurai

Sandinistas

Sanskrit

Sarekat Islam

Sassanid dynasty

savannas

schism

Schlieffen Plan

scholasticism

scientific revolution

scientific method

scribe

secularism

Second French Republic

sectionalism

sects

sedentary

seed drill

senate

Seneca Falls Convention

separate spheres

sepoys

serfs

settlement houses

Seven Years' War

shari'ah

sheikh

Shi'ah

Shinto

Shoen

shogun

Silk Roads

silt

Six-Day War

Slave Coast

smog

social Darwinism

socialism

Socratic method

solidarity

Sophists

sovereign power

sovereignty

Soviets

Spanish Civil War

spheres of influence

spinning jenny

Spring and Autumn Period

Stamp Act

standard of living

Statue of Westminster

stela

strategic bombing

stratigraphy

strike

subculture

Suez Crisis

sultan

Sunnis

Supreme Commander for
    the Allied Powers

suttee

Swahili


Taika reforms

Taiping Rebellion

Taj Mahal

Tanzimat

telescope

Ten Commandments

Tennis Court Oath

Teppes

Tet Offensive

theme system

theology

theory of Forms

Third Reich

Third Republic

third world

three-field system

Tiananmen Square Massacre

Tongzhi Restoration

topography

Torah

totalitarianism

trade imbalance

trade sanctions

trade unions

Tran-Saharan trade

Treaty of Karlowitz

Treaty of Paris

Treaty of Utrecht

Treaty of Westphalia

trenches

tribe

tribunes

Triple Alliance

Triple Entente

trusts

tsetse fly

Twelve Tribes of Israel

tyrant

U-boats

ulama

Unam sanctam

United Gold Coast Convention

United Nations

universal manhood suffrage

Upanishads

urbanization

utilitarianism

utopian socialism

Varnas

vassal

Vedas

Versailles Treaty

viceroy

Vichy France

Viet Cong

Viet Minh

vietnamization

vizier

Wafd Party

Wannsee Conference

War of Attrition

war chariot

warlords

War of the Roses

Warsaw Pact

Washington Naval Conference

water frame

Weimar Republic

welfare state

westernization

White Revolution

whites

World Trade Organization

Wu wei

Yasa

yin and yang

Young Italy movement

Young Turks

zaibatsu

zemstvos

Zen Buddhism

ziggurats

Zionism

Zollverei

# Appendix H: Developmental Stages of ELLs' English Proficiency and Vocabulary

| Language Levels | Beginning | Intermediate | Advanced |
|---|---|---|---|
| **Listening/reading comprehension** | Comprehend simple yes or no questions and simple phrases dealing with daily communication<br><br>Rely on L1 for reading comprehension of the text | Understand a lot more class discussions<br><br>Can comprehend simple stories or texts<br><br>Can follow class talks and directions and ask for help when needed | Understand both conversational and academic English well<br><br>Read grade-level-appropriate readings |
| **Speaking/writing** | Not able to speak or speak only in one word or two<br><br>Able to point, listen, draw, choose, and express meaning using facial expressions and physical movements | Can use simple phrases and sentences<br><br>Can communicate with peers and the teacher in a supported environment<br><br>Able to tell, define, compare, and summarize simple stories and write personal descriptions and short answer responses | Fluent with speaking & interaction with peers and the teacher<br><br>Able to write complex sentences and different types of writing<br><br>Able to respond to test questions in varied formats |
| **Vocabulary size** | Very basic vocabulary; about a couple hundred words | A couple thousand words | Between 3,000 and 5,000 words |
| **Teaching strategies** | Use visuals, senses, and ELLs' native language to teach vocabulary<br><br>Use simple language in class talks<br><br>Ask yes or no questions<br><br>Simplify the readings; use non-verbal assessment<br><br>Teach both basic words and academic words | Use multiple senses to teach vocabulary<br><br>Engage students in group work<br><br>Integrate simple language with academic language<br><br>Modify reading<br><br>Ask students to elaborate and support their responses in both oral and written forms<br><br>Teach both basic words and academic words | Develop academic language skills<br><br>Give reading/writing assignments and class discussions that require the skills for analysis, hypothesis, and justifying and supporting<br><br>Teach in-depth word knowledge and develop independent word-learning skills |

# INDEX

• • • • •